POETRY REVIEW

The Greeks thought of language as a veil which protects us from the brightness of things. I think poetry is a tear in that veil. – Alice Oswald

Poetry Review

Poetry Review editorial office:
The Poetry Society, 22 Betterton Street, London, WC2H 9BX
Tel: 020 7420 9883 • Fax: 020 7240 4818
Email: poetryreview@poetrysociety.org.uk
www.poetrysociety.org.uk

Editor: Maurice Riordan
Production: Michael Sims
Thanks to Sophie Kirk and Eleanor Turney

ISBN: 978-1-900771-79-5 ISSN: 0032 2156
Cover illustration by Simon Pemberton
www.simonpemberton.com

Submissions
For details of our submission guidelines,
please visit the *Poetry Review* section
of www.poetrysociety.org.uk

Advertising
To advertise, visit poetrysociety.org.uk or
contact Robyn Donaldson on 020 7420 9886,
email: marketing@poetrysociety.org.uk

Bookshop distribution
Central Books, 99 Wallis Rd, London
E9 5LN, UK. Tel: 0845 458 9925
or visit www.centralbooks.com

PBS exclusive book supply service
Poetry Review readers can receive many of
the books featured in the magazine post-free
by mail order from the Poetry Book Society.
To order, tel: 020 7831 7468, Mon-Fri,
quoting *Poetry Review*.

Subscriptions & sales
UK individuals: £34 • Europe: £44
Rest of the World: £49
(all overseas delivery is by airmail)
Single issue: £8.95 plus postage.
Order online: www.poetrysociety.org.uk, or
contact Paul McGrane on 020 7420 9881.
Pay by cheque (sterling and US dollar
cheques only), credit card or Direct Debit.

Poetry Review is also available on audio CD.

Poetry Review is the magazine of the Poetry
Society and was first published in May 1909.
It appears quarterly and is issued free to
members of the Poetry Society. The views
expressed in *Poetry Review* are not necessarily
those of the Poetry Society; those of
individual contributors are not necessarily
those of the Editor.

Charity Commission No 303334.

EDITORIAL

"An honest, descriptive, detailed, clarifying criticism keeps poetry healthy" – so wrote Douglas Dunn 20 years ago, adding "it's poetry's weedkiller". Such a cleansing notion of the role of the critic harked back to 'The Function of Criticism', T.S. Eliot's essay of 1923, which took a poor view of the impressionistic reviewing practised by the belletrists of the day. Eliot set out a more hard-headed approach and in the process laid the foundation for the New Criticism. This would eventuate in decades of sterile academic writing. But it produced, too, the great insights of I.A. Richards and William Empson, among others, and the still exemplary reviewing of Randall Jarrell. The critic's tools, Eliot proposed, were *comparison* and *analysis*, its objectives *elucidation* and the *correction* of taste.

Eliot eased up later. But I'd like to hold onto these bracing and rather punitive terms for the moment. In many respects, poetry has never been healthier: more books, pamphlets, magazines – both paper and online – are published than ever; websites offer us a cornucopia of indiscriminate material; readings of one sort or another are everywhere and fairly popular; while 'prizes' spring up like magic mushrooms. We've had a decade, too, of the proliferation of courses, workshops, creative writing degrees. True, the readership for poetry doesn't seem to have expanded in line with this activity (poetry book sales are currently on the slide). But, on the supply side, there is an abundance of publications, and a broad range of poetry available from performance through to the severely 'experimental'. This is all to the good, though if I got a pound whenever someone self-declares as a 'poet' on the radio, I suspect I wouldn't have to fly Ryanair much longer.

Isn't it about time to retrieve that drum of Paraquat from the back of the tool shed? And maybe take to including a small sample, when assigning books for review? That might eliminate "all that London undergrowth", as Larkin dismissively called it. Well, no. There's everything to be said for poetry as a democratic art. The mind loves jingles, patterns, funny noises – and the expression of emotion through a means other than tears is universal and salutary. So it's good news poetry has found its pottery equivalent, so to speak, a place where we all can have a go, play around, be amateurish and get dirty.

That said, we mustn't forget poetry is also at the limit of human capacity. It is that "tear" in the "veil" of language, as Alice Oswald puts it in her interview, that exposes us to "the brightness of things". This issue also reproduces some of the drawings of Sylvia Plath, done in the first years of her marriage to Ted Hughes. I'd be the last to romanticise Plath's early death. But poetry is risk-taking, heroic, a flight of the undaunted spirit into the unknown. Plath is rightly celebrated for her intensity, which is equally a quality of style, of that exhilarated metaphoric precision whereby language attains its most perfect and memorable expression.

There, in a word, is what has kept the show going for its few thousand years: memorability. We have no guarantee whatever that we'll add to the stock. Our age may well be a blank. But if it's not to be, then the writing of poetry needs to be attended by a scrupulous criticism, by those who set the bar according to the measure of tradition. A poem begins its life in the warmth of a mouth, and may prosper in the social context of its immediate readers and hearers. Once beyond those initial conditions, however, it will lead a lonely Darwinian existence where only the leanest and swiftest survive.

Every poem should be crafted to outlast a change of taste – if it outlasts two, it can live indefinitely, unless it meets with some physical catastrophe. The urge to cherish, then, has to be balanced by the need to discriminate. A robust poetry politic depends on a sensitive and articulate awareness of what's good. It depends, too, on critics striking an honest contract with their readers. We need a generation of those who are well informed and well disposed, but prepared to make the hard calls: judicious as well as appreciative.

The judges of the Ted Hughes Award for New Work in Poetry 2013, **Sean Borodale**, **Eileen Cooper** & **Denise Riley** invite recommendations from Poetry Society and Poetry Book Society members.

Recommendations for the 2013 award will be accepted until **6 January 2014**. For more details about the award and to download a recommendation form, visit: www.poetrysociety.org.uk/content/competitions/ tedhughes/recommend

THE POETRY SOCIETY

TED HUGHES AWARD FOR **NEW WORK** IN **POETRY**

Contents

Volume 103:4 Winter 2013

GALLERY

REVIEWS

Matthew Francis
Silverfish, Moth

after Robert Hooke, Micrographia

One swish of itself and it vanished
into the alley between two books.
There was a twilight city in there,
    leather and paper and dust,
where it had eaten itself a home.

You see it mostly going away,
a virtuoso of departure,
all tail, flickering into absence.
    Its shine is a non-colour,
the blankness of cloud in a window.

At last I had one, the tapering
torso of linked, metallic segments,
the helmet of head with four feelers,
    three more feelers on the tail –
feeling, like fleeing, is its business.

They call it bookworm. Its soil is words.
It is a fish that swims in the dry,
a full-grown caterpillar, a moth
    that flits among the pages,
having no need of wings. Unlike this

plumed moth, its four wings soft as an owl's,
a tired angel I found on my wall
in the splayed pose of proclamation.
    It was tufted all over,
body, legs, wing-stalks, even the horns,

brushes of fibres to catch the air.
The plumage differed, like that of birds,
according to the part it grew on.
    Days later I was finding
white specks lodged in my skin, moth-feathers.

Ant

after Robert Hooke, Micrographia

All afternoon a reddish trickle
    out of the roots of the beech
        and across the lawn,
a sort of rust that shines and dances.
    Close up, it proves to be ant,
        each droplet a horned
traveller finicking its way round
    the crooked geometry
        of a grass forest.
A finger felled in their path rocks them,
    amazed, back on their haunches.
        I see them tasting
the air for subtle intelligence,
    till one ventures to scale it,
        and others follow.

They are fidgety subjects to draw.
    If you sink the feet in glue
        the rest twists and writhes;
kill one, the juices evaporate
    in seconds, leaving only
        the shrivelled casing.
I dunked one in brandy. It struggled
    till the air rose from its mouth
        in pinprick bubbles.
I let it soak an hour, then dried it,
    observed the spherical head,
        the hairlike feelers,
the grinning vice of its sideways jaw,
    the coppery armour plate
        with its scattered spines.

Some draught stirred it then. It rose to all
    its feet, and set off across
        the rough miles of desk.

Harvestman, Spiderweb

after Robert Hooke, Micrographia

A head that scurries across the ground,
teetering on its scaffold of legs,
it seems a spider drawn by a child.

The eyes are back-to-back fortresses
in the middle of the domed body,
each of them commanding a half-world.

The fragile stilts, fine as eyelashes,
sway on their many joints. It hoists one,
a bent fishing-rod, testing the air.

A crab out of water, its lightness
fitted for the thinner element,
it can run on the tips of grassblades.

Ingenious contraption of legs!
The muscles are housed here, underneath,
in this cluster of cone-shaped cases.

It hunts by leaping, having no need
of the webs of more sedate spiders,
those nets they weave from some inner goo,

which I study also: the stout threads
that radiate from the heart (the warp),
the flimsier woof strung in between

with its scattering of clear globules –
spider-spittle, perhaps, or dewdrops
caught, like the rainbow light, in the mesh.

Diana Pooley
A Racehorse Undersized

He was something like a racehorse undersized...
        'The Man from Snowy River' – Banjo Paterson

Horses I'd known wouldn't let you near
in the paddock. They'd stop chewing mid-mouthful,
raise their heads, and stock-still, ears pricked,
watch as you worked your way
round clumps of Mitchell grass towards them
before they mooched off swishing their tails

so that to catch one, you'd have to use the jeep
and muster the whole mob into the round yard
near the homestead. But there was the day a stranger
showed up – a real racehorse undersized
some drover must have lost. She stayed put
and lifted her fine, chestnut nose for me to stroke.

I was twelve. She didn't buck, could jump the log
behind the shearing shed, could turn on a sixpence
and when, with my hands well down,
l touched her with my heel and leaned forward,
she would rear (her front legs tucked right up),
rear almost as high as Hopalong Cassidy's Topper.

Nice-toed, Bluff, Fresh, Nonpareil

My man knows a hat when he sees one. His
is yellow. He's good on shoes too – my sorrow:
they cover his lovely feet. Nice-toed man.

His smile is a row of suns – how his lips stretch!
He looks straight at me if I go on and on – no
nagging or womanly smart-alecking fazes him.

My man's got a click and a clack to his fingers
you'd die for. Sometimes he's bluff, sometimes
he's chic, sometimes he jiggles about. Mint mad

he is: keeps him fresh... oh, and isn't he fresh.
He can scoop me up under one arm, the kids
under the other, joggle up and down, and run

us all into the waves, or off to the Handi-Pandi
which, in our part of the world, responds well
to a fella who's not only It, but *nonpareil*.

Kim Moore
Boxer

If I could make it happen backwards
just with words, so you could start again
then I would, beginning with you
on the floor, the doctor in slow motion
reversing from the ring, the screams
of the crowd pulled back in their throats,
your coach, arms outstretched, retreats
to the corner as men get down from chairs
and tables, and you rise again, so tall,
standing in that stillness in the seconds
before you fell, and the other girl, the fighter,
watch her arm move around and away
from your jaw, and your mother rises
from her knees, her hands still shaking,
as the second round unravels itself
and instead of moving forward,
as your little Irish coach told you to,
you move away, back into the corner,
where he takes your mouth guard out
as gently as if you were his own.
The water flies like magic from your mouth
and back into the bottle and the first round
is in reverse, your punches unrolling
to the start of the fight, when the sound
of the bell this time will stop you dancing
as you meet in the middle, where you come
and touch gloves and whisper good luck
and you dance to your corners again,
your eyes fixed on each other as the song
you chose to walk into sings itself back
to its opening chords and your coach

unwraps your head from the headguard,
unfastens your gloves, and you're out
of the ring, with your groin guard,
your breast protector, you're striding
round that room full of men,
a warrior even before you went in.

Candles

after C.P. Cavafy

How fast the line of cold, dead candles grows.
Look how they put their wax heads in their hands
to weep, or fold themselves chest first towards
the floor, as if at the end of some performance.

How soon they lose their height, how soon
the black smoke rises, stopping their slow slide
along the edges of each other. They nosed
their way towards the ground with the certainty

of saints, threw the shadows of our hearts against
the walls. Now I see dead candles everywhere,
haunted by their last slow breath, their single-minded
need to burn again, to soften themselves, to ache

towards each other. Paused in this last act of falling,
they do not want to hold themselves together.

Jonathan Edwards
Girl

That girl's the girl I mean. That one now, wearing
no-animals-were-harmed-in-making-these-
leopardskin leggings, ears posing the question

of what are ears for, really,
but bearing the weight of the biggest silver-
coloured hoops on earth? In diamanté

scarlet heels, six inch,
when she walks, everything sparkles, everything
limps. Her hair is piled up on her head,

like the kind of coastal clifftop rampart
cameras swoop in at from the sea,
in historical action movies, featuring

Mel Gibson. Up her sleeve
is a tattoo, a Chinese symbol, and what it means
is clear. Look, that's her now, outside *The Mermaid*,

going a little cross-eyed as she draws
on a cigarette and shouts across the street,
asks an acquaintance if she'd like

some, would she? So how else
can I put it? How much clearer can I be?
That girl's the girl. That girl's the girl for me.

Nun on a Bicycle

Now here she comes, rattling over cobbles,
powered by her sandals, the gentle downhill
and the grace of God. Now here she comes, her habit

what it was always waiting to become:
a slipstream. Past stop signs, the pedestrian
traffic at rush hour, the humdrum mopeds,

on a day already thirty in the shade:
with her robe fluttering like solid air,
she makes her own weather. Who could blame her

as the hill sharpens, she picks up speed and smiles
into her future, if she interrupted
the *Our Fathers* she's saying in her head,

to say *Whee*, a gentle *Whee*, under her breath?
O cycle, Sister! Look at you now, freewheeling
through the air conditioning of the morning –

who's to say the God who isn't there
isn't looking down on you and grinning?

Mir Mahfuz Ali
MIG-21 Raids at Shegontola

Only this boy moves
between the runes of trees
on his tricycle
when an eagle swoops,
releases two arrows
from its silver wings and melts
away faster than lightning.
Then a loud whistle
and a bang like dry thunder.
In a blink the boy sees
his house roof sink.
Feels his ears ripped off.
The blast puffs up a fawn smoke
bigger than a mountain cloud.
The slow begonias rattle
their scarlet like confetti.
Metal slashes
the trees and ricochets.
Wires and pipes snap
at the roots, quiver.
The whirling smoke packed
with bricks and cement,
chicken feathers and nigella seeds.
When the cloud begins
to settle on the ground,
the boy makes out buckled iron rods.
White soot descends
and he finds himself dressed
like an apprentice baker.

Dog Seed

A nine-year-old scrambles out of his tin shack
to find two dogs jammed rump to rump –
a gruff mongrel with slashing jaws
dragging another up the street, a third of its size,
yowling at the grip of the knot, from which
it can't run. As the sun fries the fleas on their backs,
the boy decides to pull them apart.

So with a rogue stick he whacks the stud.
Then quick as a shuttle their frightened bodies
crash into the guy rope tethered to the ground,
tearing them from their filaments, her sex
bulbous as an injured strawberry, the inner skin
inside out, its pulp glinting between taut thighs.

The sire's virgule is an imperfect scarlet lipstick
half severed – looks as if it's been chewed.
Something milky, like gum seeds, comes out
of the gangling rod and daubs the tarmac,
its heat-odour calling to flies and ants,
the air heady with the ragged smell of release.

Susan Wicks
The Thought Snail

It drops on my desk like luck,
a small pale glob of something
next to my computer,
as if from a roosting bird
but half-transparent. Whitish. Wait –
a tentacle emerges, then another,
and it slides itself
towards my laptop, climbs the cave-mouth cliff
by the USB port, inches its way across
the Dolby label's green-and-silver leaf
to the distant mouse-pad,
crosses the left click
and hangs, its belly to the orange light
that means the battery's charging,
curls itself about
and travels like a spreading spill
of honey on the casing,
its soft shell
abraded on one side,
secreting this thin path
to another cliff-edge – and suspends itself
then plops
to land on hardwood like a ball of spit,
its wrinkled skin shrunk back
into the whorls of dark.
I search for it
and see it creeping out,
a single eyeball waving on its stalk –
then put the magnifying glass away
and try to write. I know it's here somewhere,
advancing inch by inch
towards a window, pale foot pressed
to a translucent comma,
resting in the giant shadow
of some other chair.

Kate Bingham
My Hand

I had just turned to face the door,
as usual I slept, you read,
when in a quiet voice you said
you never touch me any more.

At once I reached across the bed
but reaching felt my hand withdraw –
how many nights had I ignored
your tics and twitches, sighs and sweats

and woken shivering at dawn
my hip against the mattress edge?
The duvet held its double breath,
the pillows could not say for sure

how many nights I had instead
dismissed as a domestic chore
the tenderness we shared before,
too flat to let myself be led

across the undulating floor
of hand-me-down parquet bedspread
Granny salvaged shred by shred
in threadbare 1944,

sick of margarine and bread
and tired of waiting on the war,
of telegrams in pinafores
and bogeymen in garden sheds,

picturing in scraps of cardboard,
khaki strips and squares of red
a soldier's decorated chest,
the overcoat her husband wore.

I looked at you and as you slept
my body, suddenly too warm,
remembered what its blood was for,
my fingers tingled with regret

and reached a second time towards
your folded arms and open neck.
My lips were dry, my face was wet
but when I closed my eyes I saw

something in me not ready yet
to let me let you rest assured,
and made my hand a human claw
and clenched the air above your head.

String

The farmer kept his trousers up with string.
Out of his pockets like an entertainer
with a Punch and Judy sausage-string
he summoned knots of orange binder-twine,
a scruffy scratchy plastic nest of string
his filthy freckled hands pressed into mine.

The lining of his jacket hung in strings
but there would be a Cadbury's eclair,
a humbug, or a coil of licorice string
unraveling somewhere, hidden in the hem,

and I was not to give him back his string
until his fingers turned into a hen
and laid a sweet. He didn't need the string.
I tugged his arm and trotted after him.

Midnight

I have had too much sleep to sleep
but not enough to let me keep
tomorrow's promises and lie
awake all night. Instead of sheep

I count the faint familiar sighs
of taxi-drivers passing by.
I wonder if they've lost their way,
the roads are hard to recognise –

even our own – the houses sway
in light-polluted pavement grey.
Your breath is seasonless and slow
as aeroplanes at break of day

and when I hear your step below
my heart gets up to meet you, though
you're here with me asleep, I know,
and haven't anywhere to go.

Helen Mort
Lethal Roy

for Brendan

He's the dog you never
bet on, the one who
always, nearly, might have, will...

The one who steals the show
while no one's watching,
outrunning surprise,

or doesn't even have to run,
stitching the race up
from his kennel bed.

Dead afternoons, he pads
down the home strait,
his shadow half a pace ahead

He's the name traced
in the phone directory
twenty years too late,

the face seen for
a second on the train,
not shaken since.

When he runs,
his breathing's everything
you never said,

his fur the colour
of the last great snow,
or the colour of nothing.

FACE TO FACE

Alice Oswald

INTERVIEWED BY DERYN REES-JONES

DRJ: Do you remember the first poem that you published and the circumstances from which it arose?

AO: 'A Greyhound in the Evening after a Long Day of Rain' (*The Thing in the Gap-Stone Stile*) arrived after a year of speechlessness, during which I broke my rhyming habit and searched for a new verse form to describe gardening. In the greyhound poem, I suddenly recognised a kind of chemical bonding between syntax and tune that had all the sureness of rhyme without its bossiness; I liked its trickling, stumbling way of moving, so different from the jog-along pentameter – something as if a smashed hexameter had risen from the dead. But I couldn't quite finish the poem. I was biking back from work (after a long day of rain), when a greyhound ran out of the woods in front of me – a living description of the lightness and strangeness of the weather...

As I started thinking about the way in which your poems divide themselves between the lyrical and the narrative and the dramatic (though of course the narrative much less so), what sprang immediately to mind was Joyce writing in A Portrait of the Artist as a Young Man *when Stephen Dedalus lays out his aesthetic theory: "The lyrical form, the form wherein the artist presents his image in immediate relation to himself; the epical form, the form wherein he presents his image in mediate relation to himself and to others; the dramatic form, the form wherein he presents his image in immediate relation to others." It also made me think on from there of Virginia Woolf's* Between the Acts *and her own wrestling with genre.*

How conscious is that movement for you between lyric, epic and dramatic? Would you in any way see it as strategic?

Of course I am a Homer fanatic, so the idea of epic haunts everything I write. With their eyes on Virgil, people insist that epic has to be long and noble and nationalist and historical, but I have my own definitions and they frequently change. I find Homer anonymous, multiple, panoramic, outward-facing, fractured and shockingly, almost traumatically, alive – so that is what I aim for even in short poems. But I also find Homer both lyrical and dramatic. By lyrical I probably mean that passages in the *Iliad* are sometimes structured like a shriek (forcefully and unwastefully emotional), and by dramatic I mean full of voices and aimed at performance (though of course there is much that is undramatic about the distracted style of oral verse).

Joyce's definitions are beautiful, but once you're inside a poem those mediations and immediations are in turbulence. I try not to classify what's happened until the language has landed. Instead, I restrict myself to two forms: the Finished and the Unfinished. Under the Finished Form, I see everything measured and clear and complete and slightly delayed. Under the Unfinished Form, things look syncopated and complicated and still coming into being. I try to use both at the same time, as if they were my right eye and my left eye.

The Thing in the Gap-Stone Stile *was published in 1996, when you were 30. How long did that book take? My impression was that it happened quite quickly once you had found your voice.*

A couple of poems in that collection ('Woman in a Mustard Field' and 'Ballad of a Ghost') were written while I was 18/19, still at university. In those days I only wrote tight sonnets or loose ballads (my own kind of ballad, not narrative but stationary) and was mostly interested in that edge where the mind full of hope meets the world full of fact (and I think this is the same as the above-mentioned edge between finished and unfinished forms...). Perhaps this had as much to do with romance as philosophy. When I left university and trained as a gardener, I went on investigating that edge but the oppositions became more extreme, because I was now in constant contact with plants – extraordinary, silent, vigorous, inaccessible beings – and yet still had my head full of over-blown emotions and classical philosophy. Much of the language of that book is made of bursts of growth of loosely-linked shapes of syntax and rhythm, which was the form I found for coping with the closeness of plants. Six years into my gardening career, I got married and took a job on the North Devon coast, so there are also a lot of watery poems in there. Water taught me something about unfixity. So it goes on – the poems are just a shorthand record of the mind trying to work out its position in the world.

So there is a very direct link for you between the natural world and poetry. Poetry as organic form?

The important thing for me is that poems should be alive (actually and indefinably alive not just robotic), so I devote a lot of time to studying living forms. I want to work out how they're animated. I like Jean Christophe Bailey's idea that animals and plants are different conjugations of the verb 'to be'. If it didn't contradict what I said above about genres, I'd suggest that the lyric voice is to do with feeling and the epic voice to do with being. Anyhow, it is 'being' that I write about. Even in love poems, it is the otherness of love and not the sentiment that interests me. For that reason my poetic forms are mostly derived from the natural world. But of course a sonnet (if its connections are kept animate) can be just as 'natural' or 'organic' as free verse. But villanelles and sestinas and haikus sound so smug they always die in my hands.

Following on from that, I'm wondering about your interest in the sonnet – you've edited a selection of Wyatt's writing.

Of all the forms, the sonnet seems to me the most whole, the most locked. I treat it as a picture of thought, full of symmetries and recollections. I love its breathing movement. I love the pressure of its decorations. I love the couplet at the end of a Shakespeare sonnet, which arrives miraculously out of the language like the ghost of a Noh play. But I worry about the smoothness of sonnets. When I write them I have to crack the surface, otherwise I can only hear my own voice and what I'm always after is the voice that isn't language. For that reason, I often go for the seven-couplet style of sonnet that John Clare used. I like the way it breaks into complete pieces with breathing in between them. Wyatt's sonnets have the most beautiful rhythms of all, as if a prose voice was muttering under the poem voice. That complex, chord-like sound has influenced everything I write.

When you give a reading, you speak your poems by heart, directly from the body's rhythms, without the page as intermediary. Drawing on the ancient oral roots of poetry seems deeply bound up with your writing. Perhaps you could talk a little about this and how it ties in with your process of composition?

It isn't possible for me to be an oral poet, but I make secret curtseys to that tradition all the time. I'm always wary of picking up a pen or opening a book. I try to gather material from living things. I write with more voices than my own. I want poems to work as spoken tunes and spend a lot of energy experimenting with the notation of sound. As far as possible, when performing, I speak the work from memory. My first principle (which I keep in mind whenever I write) is that oral traditions are unfinished and therefore still malleable, still alive to the present moment.

I feel as if I write on the run, ducking into doorways, hiding in sheds, packing everything into a biro and vanishing, stealing thoughts, living several lives at once. It's hard to concentrate when there are children around, but I work when I can in a shed behind a compost heap. I don't write straight onto a computer. I get up very early, I draw things out on paper and if I'm stuck I walk. I'm very practised at working on poems while doing other things. I think the real matter of a poem is everything that takes shape without a pen or computer.

Of course oral composition bears no resemblance to this. An oral poet learns a metrical language which he can then speak spontaneously. I have an image of the great oral poems lying like a layer of mist above the earth. So my ambition is not so much to 'compose' poems, more to translate or hear or inhale or partake of them.

Writing 'on the run' has its good and bad aspects. I can see very much it's about the pressures of time, particularly those that affect you as a parent. But as a metaphor for movement, the "unfixity" you talked about in relation to water, it sounds to me very positive! And you have, in fact, numerous poems in which walking figures, including the title poem of Woods *etc., when you write of walking and the body and writing as a kind of simultaneous act. My sense is that it is rare, in British women's poetry, for there to be a moving, embodied female self in a poem. Do you think that walking trope becomes a bigger metaphor for a mobile self who can move between and from voice to voice?*

The walking is actual. It's a good way of stabilising thinking. Rather than being a "metaphor for a mobile self", walking gives the self continuity through time. In fact in the poem you mention, which describes a day lost in trees on Dartmoor, walking was the only proof it was still me among those huge, anonymous, increasing woods. So I normally work a thread of movement through the fragments of a poem, because I like to hear the friction of coherence and incoherence rubbing together. But it requires quite a lot of energy to keep those forces in balance. Poems are literally made of breath. When I was writing *Memorial* I took to running at night as a way of developing stamina. That seemed the only way to sustain the evenness of the verse. I don't know about other women. I've always felt the strength of Emily Brontë's poems came from walking.

I'm fascinated by this. I wonder whether the movement being 'actual' stops it also allowing you to find a lyrical self which isn't frozen or compartmentalised or constrained? Is that something you strive for? Your interest in fluidity, perhaps the deconstructing of binaries, reminds me how a similar impulse, albeit a very different style, works in Jo Shapcott's writing. For her this often focuses on gender. Would being thought about as a woman poet be something you would not think about or would wish to avoid?

Perhaps women can only speak honestly (un-manipulatively) once they are rid of the constraints of identity. Certainly I prefer not to have a gendered image of myself when writing, so that I can find the voices I use when there's no one else around. I take seriously what Blok said of Akhmatova – that she "writes poems as if a man is watching her, but you have to write as if God is watching". But when I'm not writing, I'm proudly female and feminist or at least conscious of the need for someone to speak back to the male cultural megaphone.

There's a wonderful clip on YouTube of you reading from Rockaby, *and you have spoken publicly about Beckett being important to you, describing him as a "pinhole writer" "who created a darkroom of language through which, in spite of himself, light passes". I can see very much your engagement with ideas of repetition and rhythm coming out of an engagement and enjoyment of his work, but rather than being flavoured by Beckett's nihilism, his movement always towards death, your poems always strike me as celebratory, not so much caught in the repetitions as buoyed up, sustained by them. Is that fair?*

The context of any poem is Time (the poem either runs with it or pretends to interrupt it, but in both cases depends on its steadiness) and Beckett is for me the best interpreter of Duration. He never loses track of it. If I use repetition it's neither celebratory nor nihilistic, but a quick way of alluding to this musical, exact context. But anyway, because he's a dramatist, Beckett's work always has something else other than language going on. Often it takes the form of light – for example moonlight or twilight or the switching on and off of lamps. I like this doubleness. I would never describe him as nihilist, because of the silent humorous presence of the physical world subverting whatever he (or his characters) sets out to say. Also, there is so much Dante in Beckett, all his images carry a certain after-world or inter-world glow.

Perhaps you can say some more here about that idea of Time and Duration – which comes from Bergson as a concept, doesn't it?

It's hard to talk about time except through poetry, which can so easily (by means of rhythm) keep past, present and future on the same plane, creating a kind of technical or magical time – which allows the gaps in the verse, through which real time is audible, to express something that can't be expressed in prose – so no, I'd better not try!

And humour, that's actually a big part of some of your writing, a playful, resilient quality that gives a direct line to the unconscious?

Clumsiness is quite a problem for me. More than most people I seem to bump into things and catch clothes on door handles and drop glasses. So my poems, if they're being honest, will normally show some trace of the Spirit of Slip-up.

Your second collection, Dart, *is a book-length poem, constructed out of a series of interviews with the people who lived and worked on the river. In that poem the voices of all the people and the river become one. In* Woods etc. *your poems 'Leaf' and 'Wood Not Yet Out' use the image of a leaf that has not yet come into bud as a metaphor for a pregnancy, but what happens in that poem is that the leaf becomes the baby and the baby becomes the leaf. The poem is a kind of Gestalt duck-rabbit. How do you see that divide between the human and nature, nature and culture?*

The imagination is a sense that sees connections not divisions. Once you open the imagination's eye, everything looks like something else. And language, whose roots belong to a great network of metaphors, is a record of almost infinite shape-shifts, which the rhymes and re-windings of poetry make more visible. For me, the challenge when writing is not to surrender completely to that force, but to push the rational mind against it: to be able to see things from their own perspectives but also to see their divisions and distinctions, singularities, shadows, sealed worlds, edges, separations, blocks, fine lines, free nouns, unhitched conjunctions. So in answer to your question, I see the divide strobe-lit: it is there and not there, there and not there...

In Weeds and Wild Flowers *you collaborated with the artist Jessica Greenman. What was the original impulse behind that collaboration?*

It was more of a conversation than a collaboration, much of it conducted by telephone. I originally hoped that Jessica's images would correspond exactly to the named plants, but it became clear after a while that it was more interesting if neither of us illustrated the other. So we worked separately but sometimes Jessica, who lives in London, came and drew the plants that grow in Devon. I was inspired by the precision of her line (which you don't really see in the printed reproductions) and by her informed and obsessive and eccentric understanding of flowers.

Clare's wildflower poems, his relationship with the natural world, what John Barrell has described as Clare's "aesthetics of disorder", must have informed that project?

I love Clare's aesthetics, but *Weeds and Wild Flowers* is light-hearted and has more to do with speaking up for lost internal voices than with painstakingly watching the natural world. The main text I used was Keble Martin's flower guide. He was a nineteenth-century vicar who lived for a while on the Dartington Estate and recorded the local flowers. I had the sense that his patient scrutiny of the ground allowed him to describe many of the local ghosts without noticing.

We often hurl out the Auden line about poetry making nothing happen while forgetting how he goes on to say that poetry is "a way of happening, a mouth". Do you see a direct connection between your writing and a more obviously ideological green politics?

I wouldn't say that my poems are trying to express something "green" but perhaps that my politics are trying to express something I've learnt through poetry, which is after all a government (or grammar) of internalised characters. I think "green" questions are often confused with conservation questions, when really they have more to do with justice and self-government. I'm wary of the temptation to write a kind of gated green poetry that simply mourns and remembers.

In Memorial, *your most recent collection, you offer a free translation of the* Iliad. *Can you remember the particular moment when you sat down and thought you were going to tackle the* Iliad *and why?*

All my poems are in some way translations of the *Iliad*. I'm afraid there were practical reasons for writing *Memorial*, which probably kicked the poem into being. I wanted to apply for an AHRC grant and thought a "selective translation of the *Iliad*" sounded suitably academic. I didn't get the grant but wrote it anyway.

There often comes a point for poets, around their third or fourth book, when there seems to be an impulse to write a novel. I imagine this isn't the case for you, in fact, given what we've been talking about in relation to the epic and poetry?

The trouble with novels is that they aren't designed to be performed and I'm never satisfied until I hear the physical, breath-driven force of language turning into voice.

I remember reading that you don't really look to contemporary poets in your reading, or at least, not at the beginning. Has that changed as your work has developed?

I'm afraid I still read rather medicinally, looking for a precise taste or tincture, and when I find the text that provides it I just study that and nothing else, which means I'm quite ill-informed about literature in general. For example, I haven't spent a lot of time on Auden or Browning and I admit I don't have a very clear picture of contemporary poetry, although I'm excited by the glimpses I catch of poets (especially younger more computer-literate poets) with very different preoccupations to my own.

People have been keen to pick up on the influence of Ted Hughes... do you find as your work develops that that engagement with another poet has changed significantly?

There was a time when I was drinking Hughes every day, but now I have the alcoholic's privilege of only needing a small amount to top up my levels. I keep him in the shed and it's sometimes enough just to look at the cover of the book to remind myself what the world really is. He was an extraordinary poet and alive in my lifetime, which means a lot to me.

Can you talk about the importance of translation to you? That space between languages, cultures, that happens in translation, ties very much into the in-between space, the space where things move and breathe, which you find in The Thing in the Gap-Stone Stile, *later emerging in* Memorial *as a full-blown response to a text in another language.*

While working on *Memorial*, I discovered two ways of translating – either I could operate on the level of words, sitting among dictionaries and exchanging one term for another, or I could go down to the level of things. This was much more difficult. It required me to stare through the Greek word at what lay behind it and translate or transmit or impersonate that. I called this method 'translucence' because Homer's world gives off a pale green light, which I wanted to let through into contemporary language. Perhaps all poetry presents these options. I react strongly against poems that are opaque (I often write them myself). The Greeks (sorry to go on about them) thought of language as a veil which protects us from the brightness of things. I think poetry is a tear in that veil.

Words and Things. This makes me think of imagism and the thinginess of things, but you are also thinking 'through' Plato here too? And Shelley's Plato when he talks of the act of translation being as wise as casting "a violet into a crucible that you might discover the formal principle of its colour and odour"? Shelley, of course, also sees poets famously as legislators of the world, who bring beneficial change to the world. Perhaps it is too much of a poetic cliché, but if poetry is, which I very much think it is, a place of and for transformation, is it also too a healing art? You used that word "medicinal" earlier in relation to your own reading, for example.

Is poetry healing? That depends what you think is broken. Poetry loosens the identities of things, which is why its voice is so companionable to people in a state of transition or loss – companionable but not comforting and perhaps not healing. In fact, its way of simultaneously expressing both the actual and its negative can be terrifying, but survival requires something precisely that sharp.

As for transformation, it only works if the poet herself has been prepared to transform – and that takes courage. In fact, I think poems are entirely a question of courage. Once you commit to them, you have to accept any dare that comes your way, otherwise you'll be writing dead poems for years. The living poems (the healing ones) are the ones that have cost you something.

Memorial asks us to remember – the text in a ghostly way keeps remembering *itself; it also prompts remembering of the recent war dead. Was there ever a temptation for you to transpose the* Iliad *into a purely contemporary setting?*

I don't know what this question means because to me the dead are entirely contemporary. I toyed with the idea of adding a tail-piece to commemorate recent wars, but the effect would have been to historicise the *Iliad* – to kill it. I want people to relate the poem to Iraq, but the various anachronisms in the text (backwards as well as forwards) are not some kind of intellectual manipulation – they are there because the original poem is not of one date, is not in time at all.

We touched on nihilism earlier and your sense of feeling neither nihilistic nor celebratory, and I wonder the extent to which your engagement with the natural world is connected with a wider spiritual sense?

Good question but difficult word. I'd rather talk about an anti-social sense than a spiritual one, because I'm very interested in what happens when you take off your hood of human voices and hear what else has been speaking. Plants in particular are points of entry to a quite different way of knowing. Even cows – I recently realised that cows, when they look at you, have no self-image of their own and therefore see through to the part of you that has never seen itself. As for grass, it seems to notice only the most lowly, resilient, whispering level of the human. These kinds of questions have nothing to do with theism and atheism. They are questions about finished and unfinished views of the mind. I suppose that's the starting-point for my 'spiritual sense' – the suspicion that the mind is unfinished and perhaps infinite.

I wonder where having finished Memorial *leaves you poetically? Do you have new work in progress?*

Yes, I'm still rabbitting on I'm afraid.

Deryn Rees-Jones is the author of *Consorting with Angels: Essays on Modern Women Poets* (Bloodaxe, 2005) and several collections of poems, including *Burying the Wren* (Seren, 2012).

∽

TS Eliot outside Faber & Gwyer.

Sunday 12 January 2014

TS Eliot Prize Readings

Hear the best contemporary poets reading their own work at one of the most prestigious poetry awards in the world. Shortlisted poets are:

Helen Mort
Robin Robertson
Sinéad Morrissey
Maurice Riordan
Daljit Nagra
Dannie Abse
Michael Symmons Roberts
George Szirtes
Anne Carson
Moniza Alvi

Royal Festival Hall
7pm

BOOK TICKETS
SOUTHBANKCENTRE.CO.UK
/LITERATURE

SOUTHBANK CENTRE

ARTS COUNCIL ENGLAND

Omphalos

I would begin with the Greek word, omphalos, *meaning the navel,
and hence the stone that marked the centre of the world, and repeat
it,* omphalos, omphalos, omphalos, *until its blunt and falling music
becomes the music of someone pumping water at the pump outside
our back door.* — Seamus Heaney, 'Mossbawn'

As part of an occasional series, we ask poets to write about their *omphalos*, a place
central to their imaginative world.

℘

Paul Farley

Thinking about a 'first place', maybe a brief assemblage of images
and half-ideas can be made to roost neatly on the page, though in
practice they'd always form more of an unsettled flock.

*

At the mouth of the Albert Dock, where the Mersey sloshes against the sea
wall, you can still see depth markers, Latin numerals carved deep into the
granite. My dad pointed these out to me when I was a kid, in the derelict
lull between Liverpool's heyday as a port and its reinvention as somewhere
else entirely. I didn't know then that the Ordnance Survey had once used
those docks as its benchmark for sea level everywhere, the absolute datum
point. Though even by the time I was taken to look, this measure had long
since slipped its moorings and drifted elsewhere.

*

But everything was always moving on, or away, or changing. Liverpool:
City of Change and Challenge it said on council letterheads and the sides
of buses. At first, I had an urban childhood, a series of dark rooms with
views onto silvery sidings in moonlight, a Giacometti of rooftop aerials,
streets with back entries and weedy wasteground. There was always the
river, where all the roads seemed to converge, this grey-green, ancient,
muddy thing: a constant presence. You could smell it. And then we were
moved, to an estate out on the edge of the city. Our 'street' – more like a

looping circuit diagram now – was the last before the city boundary. Childhood took a new and interesting turn.

*

This happened all over, quietly, to a whole swathe of the population, making up in sheer scale and numbers for what it might have lacked in urgency. Families were relocated and whole areas demolished in their wake. I remember it being referred to as decanting. I wonder now whether it set in motion a nostalgia in me that ran counter to any yearning for a more traditional Eden or idyll. I missed the city. I missed its dirtiness and its textures, its age and accretions. I remember missing it at a tender age. We'd been decanted, but some sediment remained.

*

An image of uprootedness: the house we were allocated was so newbuild I watched as a lorry came and tipped its load of earth into what was to become our back garden. Everything smelt of paint, fresh-cut timber, putty, glue, and beyond this were older smells of soil and silage, wildflowers, a leafy, grassy scent in the heat of that summer we arrived. Our garden might have literally fallen off the back of a lorry, but it proved subsistence enough. We dug up dahlia tubers in the autumn, dusted them with sulphur and placed them in the dark of the meter cupboard under the stairs. For a few winters, this felt like the centre of the house.

*

There's a metaphor for memory in one of Socrates's dialogues with Theaetetus where the mind is compared to a kind of birdcage: "let us now make in each soul an aviary stocked with all sorts of birds, some in flocks apart from the rest, others in small groups, and some solitary, flying hither and thither among them all." Lying in bed, listening to sparrows scratching under the soffit boards and starlings calling in the roofscape, I felt a kind of levitation in realising just how provisional everything was; how, only a few seasons earlier, these sparrows would have had no houses to nest in, the starlings only open fields and clumps of woodland. I lay floating in air, surrounded by birds of knowledge and birds of ignorance.

*

If I look dead straight at the idea of an *omphalos*, then the river itself might be one kind of centre or source. I occasionally still dream about it. I picture myself trying to cling to the stone sea wall, but it's too slippery and weedy. The river has a ferry, well known in a pop cultural sense, but don't let that occlude all the other, older resonances of taking a ferry across the water.

*

Records, television, cinema... I can't remember a time before. These things permeated our daily lives, as intangible as broadcasts from another planet, but in the air and on our tongues. Heaney's description of *omphalos* has a lovely, persuasive telescoping of the very local and the mythic, of two cultures. Though growing up a few decades earlier, he was certainly already alert and receptive to the wider currents flowing through the local, especially in terms of radio: think of his seventh Glanmore sonnet, or 'A Sofa in the Forties', with its "absolute speaker" of BBC RP blowing in from over the water. In how many subtle ways must these things adjust the bonds between people and places, our identities?

*

Omphalos, omphalos, omphalos... A repeated sound, a call. I recall hearing a story about a sound recordist who visited an old shattered cottage, and the strange song he encountered there of the starlings that haunted its broken slates. Starlings are great mimics, and the calls of this particular clan seemed wheezily mechanical, metallic, repetitive. After looking around for a while, the soundman found a possible source: a rusted water pump, long since seized up, but perhaps once familiar to the birds, whose ancestors might have discovered in it a squeaky anthem, or irresistible phrase, and handed it down.

Tom Sleigh

If I had an *omphalos*, it wouldn't be a place, it would be a book. When I was in first grade, and living in Utah in a tiny town high up in the Wahsatch range, my mother gave me D'Aulaire's *Book of Greek Myths* – a picture book for kids retelling the old stories. I'll never forget the picture of Cronos devouring his children. He had one of them clutched like a popsicle stick in his fist, his mouth opening to bite off the child's head. It was all graphically real, heightened from life, of course, but thoroughly recognisable as paradigmatically parental. The look on Cronos's face was part disgust, part this-is-going-to-hurt-me-worse-than-it's-going-to-hurt-you. A phrase that chimed with what my mother said on one of the very few occasions when I was spanked by my father: not a serious spanking, just a few whacks that I managed to cut short by immediately bursting into tears squeezed out with a lot of operatic wailing.

And at school, Cronos seemed like the incarnation of my math teacher, Mr Capener, a giant, florid man – slow-speaking, terminally polite, immensely patient with us, unless he caught us messing around. But none of us did mess around, because Billy Gallegos, a fearless, chubby boy who had the moral strength of the old martyrs, did it for us. Mr Capener always called us by our formal Christian names. And Mr Capener would say, with great deliberation and gravitas, "Now William, William, please pay attention." And when Billy, class clown and rebel, would continue to grab-ass around, Mr Capener's face would flush a shade darker, the colour rising in his cheeks like mercury in a thermometer. His big square jaw would work up and down, his eyes would almost cross and then he'd take Billy by the collar and throw him against the wall – an event that sometimes happened once or twice a class.

The rest of us, meanwhile, hunkered down at our desks, titillated by the violence, but feeling something like that moment in *Casablanca* when Victor Laszlo stands up and tells the band in Rick's nightclub, "Play the Marseillaise, play it!" – and all the patrons begin to sing it at the top of their lungs, drowning out the SS singing 'Die Wacht am Rhein'.

Of course, Mr Capener was nothing like a Nazi – a model teacher in most ways – and we certainly weren't little Victor Laszlos. But we cheered on Billy's rebellion in our coward hearts, while sitting silent and numb, clutching our pencils. I remember feeling exalted by the way Billy always got up laughing, which I suppose is why Laszlo comes to mind. Billy was an image of the unbowed spirit, Prometheus nailed to the cliff, flipping the bird to the birds eating his liver.

This bizarre combination of school day routine and wildly fluctuating emotion could be laid out against the grid of the myth, just as the image of Mr Capener could be superimposed on Cronos. Of course, an art buff will already have caught my mistake: there is no picture of Cronos eating his children in D'Aulaire's – that's a Goya painting that I superimposed on my past. But it's a telling mistake, so I'll let it stand.

Anyway, in my version of D'Aulaire's, there's a picture of a stone wrapped in baby clothes that Cronos swallows, thinking it's his son, Zeus, whom he's afraid will overthrow him. Of course, Cronos himself overthrew his father, Uranus, by cutting off his balls with a sickle given him by his mother, Gaia. And so the family drama continues: Zeus's wife gives Cronos poison, and he vomits up Zeus's other brothers and sisters – including the stone – that he devoured before Zeus. He and his sibs rise up against their father and imprison him in Tartarus. Afterwards, they place the stone at Delphi, the original *omphalos*.

Events in my house weren't nearly so gory, but shifting allegiances and betrayals were all part of our family dynamics. And the story also made sense geographically: on the mountain side above our town was a giant B made out of boulders painted white (the B stood for Box Elder County) – the navel to our tiny, isolated town. And on another, murkier level, I remember a hog being castrated, its gut-bucket stereophonic squealing, and the weird joking that went on among the men – the myth resonated in ways I couldn't have articulated at that age, but which nonetheless I understood emotionally all the way to the bottom: and as T.S. Eliot once said, the bottom is a long way down. (So far down, in fact, that a friend said she doubted D'Aulaire's would have included the story about the castrating sickle. But again, I think my slip is more revealing than hewing to the literal.)

And since we lived in a deer-hunting town, and often saw deer strapped to the bumpers of our neighbours' vehicles during deer season, the story of Actaeon, a hunter changed into the very prey he is hunting, also made a perverse kind of sense.

I remember Actaeon crouched behind some bushes stealing a peek at a naked woman bathing in a pool – the virgin goddess Diana – though what a virgin actually was would have been a sketchy concept for me then. Actaeon's three-quarter profile looks a little squeamish and then that squeamishness gives way on the facing page to rolling-eyed terror when you see him caught halfway in his transformation, nose thickening to a muzzle, fur sprouting all over his face, arms and legs, a pair of antlers branching from his head as his faithful dogs turn on him and chase him through the underbrush. In his half-human, half-animal heart, does he feel the terror of a buck strung up by its hooves and dripping blood from a knife slash in its throat before it's skinned out and gutted by a guy like Nick Topick? – an otherwise mild-mannered insurance agent who served as our chaperone, and whom we terrorised with hurled spitballs, on a town school bus that transported for free any kid who could squeeze a dollar out of his parents for a rope-tow pass up at Beaver Mountain.

Actaeon, of course, gets dragged down by his own dogs and eaten. I confess, I always thought Actaeon had it coming, that the deer in Nick Topick's back yard had finally taken revenge. I entirely missed the point of Diana being defiled by human eyes and desires – but I was a tamped-down kid in those days, and my sexual desires kept well below the horizon line. Nonetheless, the reversal of fate at the core of the myth made complete sense to me: just like the cartoons of deer dressed up in red hunting vests, and carrying rifles, strapping a human to the bumper of their pick-ups.

As I age, and my memory grows more unreliable, I tell myself that my lapses are the surest sign that the old stories retain their power to centre me in the world. The images, in their complex web of association, allow me to connect emotions and sensations that I otherwise couldn't comprehend. So Cronos and Mr Capener and Billy, Diana and Actaeon, and Nick, once they entered the force field of the myths, all that was inchoate and contradictory in daily life snapped into a pattern – just the way a magnet placed under a sheet of construction paper makes a pile of iron filings shape into petals around an invisible centre.

The Kids' Stuff

DAVID HARMER

It's nine in the morning, maybe a little later as it depends on Reception arriving on time. Year 6 have put out chairs and benches and sit at the back of the hall. In front is the rest of the school surrounded by the grown ups. An enthusiastic but hoping-for-the-best-because-I-have-actually-never-met-him-hope-he's-good-coz-my-budget-is-on-the-line-hardworking teacher introduces me. They say, "Good-morning, David". Only I know what is going to happen next.

Is this the moment to reach for the Inspirational and Sensitive Book Of Poems for Wee Kiddies Translated Badly From The World of the Adult, with perhaps a verse or two about an amusing cat (such fun!), a fish who is really a Spirit of The Woodland (imagine that boys and girls), or a terribly tasteful sonnet accompanied by a lute? No. It is time for the one about the cook who mixes treacle tart with glue, the teacher who pokes pencils down his ear, the mad headteacher who has a suit so stiff it creaks as he patrols the corridors, the pirates who may have parrots (it being alliteration Monday) but also have smelly feet, the monster who is banging at the door, the alien hiding in the loo, the Super Baddy known as Stinkerman and the teacher who is really from Mars. As for playing the lute, only try it if you are Paul Cookson, who strums a pretty efficient ukulele.

Almost all the poems rhyme (I owe a debt to Masefield and, of course, Kit Wright). They each have a chorus that everybody joins in, they often have a load of volunteers (pirate crews, Stinkerman and Smell-Boy) and they seem to make everybody laugh. Poetry is fun, it is loud, it is immediate, it is easy to read and hear, it has a place in a busy primary school day. Big bright colours begin to bash about.

In the middle of this, there's a poem about the school bully who is scared of swimming. It is serious in an accessible way and, oddly, it doesn't rhyme. It has no chorus. It's a poem for the page that can work out loud. So poetry can also explore serious issues; it can take the weight of children's concerns and their world, one typified by kids doing their level best to negotiate a system dominated by the adults who make no sense, a kind of random universe where the grown ups (many of whom are also trying to make sense of it) have power.

We make up big class poems that don't have to rhyme, we look at models of different styles and ranges of poetry, we have yet more fun and the children have frameworks they can use to make their own poems with at another time. In most schools, there are some collections of poetry: Roger McGough, Carol Ann Duffy, Jackie Kay, Valerie Bloom, John Foster, John Agard, Kit Wright, Michael Rosen and others. Often these books are published by Gaby Morgan at Macmillan, who continues to ensure there is a supply of exciting, brilliantly illustrated books of poems for primary-aged children.

Back to the classroom. There is a need to support colleagues in schools and provide training for poetry to flourish. Models exist. Last year the poet Roger Stevens and I worked with the Poetry Society, the National Foundation for Educational Research (NFER) and Bishop Grosseteste University College in Lincoln on a year-long project, devising with student teachers how best to introduce reading and writing poems into the primary classroom. Called Poetry Train, its final report is long and thorough.[1] Here are the key findings:

> The student teachers who participated in Poetry Train demonstrated significantly greater improvement in knowledge of and enthusiasm for poetry, confidence in teaching poetry, and acquisition of teaching skills than a comparison group.

Obviously, the aim was to work with the students and not specifically the children, although interestingly, the report found a small but significant upward shift in the children's responses as well. The project was prompted by a perception that Ofsted found little poetry in primary schools, which might be a reflection upon the knowledge and enthusiasms of the teachers. Personally, I feel it has much more to do with the pressure on schools to negotiate a minefield of ever-changing tests, targets and high jumps, consequently marginalising poetry by accident. But perhaps poetry is, like dance, art, clay and drama, one of those areas where teachers might feel put off by poor experiences when they were at school, or by the general perception that poetry is boring, difficult, and written by bearded men who wear capes and tall felt hats.

When I work in schools my aim is to inspire pupils to gain a sense of

---

1. Poetry Train was a one-year training programme designed by the Poetry Society to support student teachers going on to teach in primary schools. It was supported by funding from the Esmée Fairbairn Foundation and the Paul Hamlyn Foundation. See Cooper, L., Stevens, E., and Sainsbury, M. (2012), *An evaluation of Poetry Train*, 2011-12, Slough: NFER.

poetry, for them to want to hear, read and write poems, to have fun with language, as well as begin to explore the sensitive and profound areas of their lives. Children do not need an erudite definition of what poetry is, they simply need to know it when they see it. Here are two useful comments: Leonard Cohen described poetry as "the stuff I write with a lot of white spaces round the edges". A boy in Year 2 once told me "poems are a list". Both definitions point out that poetry is written in lines and has a different rhythm from prose, although I agree that there are very many poets who write better lists than me.

Poetry offers another way of looking at things, using all the dazzling varieties of English that are available to us and, as a bonus, children love it. They respond so well to the essential rhythms and beats of poetry, even the stuff that never rhymes. Very young children are often taught Nursery Rhymes (those cruel horror stories that smash up big talking eggs and inspire arachnophobia, the verse equivalent of Beatrix Potter's gardener eating rabbits in a pie and rats rolling cats into a roly poly pudding). The teacher is asking the child to explore the world, often very simply, as they perceive it. To do this as poets, the children will use rhythm, metaphor, alliteration, onomatopoeia, simile, symbol, image and sometimes rhyme, all within a structure. However simple these elements are, they are the stuff of poetry.

In Foundation and Key Stage 1, there is an emphasis on action, straightforward ideas, beat and bounce, and employing simple frameworks that can help with structure, before knowledge and confidence take over. The same is true of Key Stage 2, but then certain recognised forms become available. However, it's important that children do not see the various suggested models as an end in themselves, but as part of an increasing repertoire that can be developed and used for their own purposes. For example, haiku and tanka are useful ways of learning about imagery, and are concise and syllabically defined. However, it would be a great waste if children did not expand from these and write their own poetry loosely based upon these models but not worrying too much about syllabic count or the number of lines used.

Successful writing will develop most where it is valued within the school's culture, where poetry is written, read, performed and shared by the whole community, irrespective of ability, gender, ethnicity or religious belief. There is a valuable role for ICT (Information and Communication Technology) here for publishing and presenting the work to the rest of the school, as well as accessing the Poetry Society's site for schools, which is crammed with material to establish poetry in classrooms.

In fact, nearly all the adults I work with would agree poetry is important, and that if you make it fun you can establish it in the school and then go on to explore rather more demanding work than the issues offered by Stinkerman. And there are some great practitioners around, all of whom know that writing for children is a discrete form with many unique conventions, and it doesn't equal badly-written-stuff-for-adults. However (Level 5 connective), there are Dark Figures looming behind all literacy work (and much else) in schools, figures who are busily destroying creativity, insisting on overteaching the easily testable and making the overburdened lives of teachers more impossible. The Dark Figures have joined forces with the spirits of Franz Kafka and Salvador Dali to make the education system so complicated and bizarre that the route map through it is a forest of elephants, beetles and dripping tubas. It is now ten past nine and I can see them lurking at the back of the hall. They'd better watch out – Stinkerman is on their case.

Children's Poetry: a very short reading list
Anthologies
A First Poetry Book, chosen by Pie Corbett and Gaby Morgan (Macmillan Children's Books, 2012)
A Laureate's Choice, 101 Poems for Children, chosen by Carol Ann Duffy (Macmillan Children's Books, 2012)
Green Glass Beads: A Collection of Poems for Girls, chosen by Jacqueline Wilson (Macmillan Children's Books, 2012)
Michael Rosen's A-Z: The best children's poetry from Agard to Zephaniah (Puffin, 2009)
The Oxford Book of Children's Poetry, edited by Michael Harrison and Christopher Stuart-Clarke (OUP, 2007)
Poetry Jump-up: An Anthology of Black Poetry, compiled by Grace Nichols (Puffin, 1990)
Read Me and Laugh: A funny poem for every day of the year, chosen by Gaby Morgan (Macmillan Children's Books, 2005)
The Works, chosen by Paul Cookson (Macmillan Children's Books, 2004-2010)

Individual books
Carol Ann Duffy, *New and Collected Poems for Children* (Faber, 2010)
John Foster, *The Poetry Chest* (OUP, 2007)
Roger McGough, *An Imaginary Menagerie* (Puffin, 1990)
Michael Rosen, *You Wait Till I'm Older Than You* (Puffin, 2008)
Kit Wright, *The Magic Box: Poems for Children* (Macmillan Children's Books, 2013)
Cookson, Harmer, Moses, Stevens, *The Truth About Teachers* (Macmillan Children's Books, 2013)

Classroom resources
www.poetrysociety.org.uk/content/education

David Harmer is a children's author. His collections of poems for children include *Pirate Poems* (Macmillan, 2007).

Paul Farley
The Gadget

An algorithm yoked to a smart microphone
means it can throw my voice. (Years ago, this meant
the cutting out of a comic book coupon
down the dotted line, a postal order sent
to a PO Box on the Avenue of the Americas
where every handshake buzzed and sea monkeys swam;
on the wing and a prayer of knowing what a 'zip code' was,
in the hope the whole thing wasn't an elaborate scam.)
Is that me, trapped in the anchorhold of a post box?
Is that me, in my own pocket, on ringtone?
This is more fun than black soap or x-ray specs.
I laugh on the edge of the centre of attention.

But the gadget can be serious and tactical.
It can throw a thousand lumens and singe eyebrows.
It ships with an optional anodised strike bezel
and defends itself with an avian shrill that could "rouse
Saint Michael the Archangel's flapping host"
according to the literature. More practical
perhaps is the way it calculates how lost
I'd be without it, and chirrups reminders, missed calls.
I'd tell you its name, but then you might guess my password.
I'd tell you its name, but it won't recognise your voice.
If found, it will thrum in your hand like a frightened bird
as it arms itself and becomes a small device.

Can yours do this? Positioned at my temple
its alchemic palladiums and golds
excite me, bringing pleasure. Or, with a simple
click it can open a vein in spring lancet mode.
Box of sobs, bearer of pipesmoke, putty,
the inkiness of a comic read by torchlight,
it can dowse a water main in the darkest city,
and I've wondered if it feels me feeling sorry for it;
this thing that fits in my hand but can never outlive me,
this thing that sulks on standby facing the iron pole
of the planet, that knows my blood type and taste in pornography.
It points towards the presence of a soul.

Gerard Smyth
How Goes the Night

It goes like this: sleepless since
the thumping beat of a car-stereo
broke the peace and headlight beams
crossed the ceiling, going east
then disappearing in the corner
where the spider lives.

Idle thoughts, erotic longings;
a list of tasks to think about –
but no lush soundtrack to sweeten the dark
in the theatre of the mind
just the vigil of a digital clock
watching with the red eyes of a god.

Sheenagh Pugh
His Colours

He sports the jester's coat,
red and yellow;

he is all in a glow
of falling leaves, bonfires

that throw out splinters
of light. His feet crush

berries into a blood-splash
on the paving stones.

His colours: slanting suns,
clouds briefly ablaze,

he comes as a surprise,
this flaunting dandy

whom we had looked to see
in a plain black suit.

Staying

The ground beneath our feet
is shifting, has been on the move

for ever. This fissured sea-cliff
travelled north from the equator;

its heights were once an ocean floor.
Ice carves out rock, forests harden

to diamond as the stars burn down:
there is nothing that is not on a journey,

no abode for those who long only
to stay. We could be at ease

with so little, if it were for always:
a moment, a loved place. How modest

this aim to go nowhere, this least
of wishes, not to change our state.

Neil Wenborn
Longshore drift

1.

What you find
looking at beaches
is that the pebbles are graded
neatly by volume as if through a set of filters,

the smallest trickling
with sandgrains down at the tideline,
the largest up by the sea wall as if of a mind
to scale it.

Not only pebbles either. See
how the detritus of harbourwork and stopover
is sequenced –
half-smoked cigarettes,

tarred coils of rope, crushed plastic, cans – by wave upon wave
retreating
as a man might shake
dross through sieve after sieve, or how

from shellfire
ninety years ago
the colour of my eyes slipped through
the crosshairs of a German gun somewhere in Flanders.

2.

    Shufflings of shingle,
  shufflings of genes and circumstance.
From here, wherever you look you can see its workings:
     longshore drift

  setting its shoulder to the wheel
of hungering gulls, its grindstone strength against the vast
     inertia
   of land and history.

Fire up this coin-op telescope and there's time enough
     to glimpse it
   in the distant blink
  of a light-vessel, the shifting

     mid-Channel
    signatures of bar
   and sandbank, there's time to frame it
making and breaking trade routes, ships, fortunes, prospecting,

    moving towns along
  like vagrants, just time to focus
before, with a shock of falling metal, everything
     shuts to black.

3.

   So purposeful it looks, close up,
like water micromanaging the land. But now stand
      back a bit,
    let your eyes adjust

to the ebb and flow, the endless heedless argument
      of swash and
    backwash, as they might
  to darkness, and you start to see

    below it
   not the undertow
 of grief, or faith withdrawing, no
metaphor of advance and loss, but gravity, just

    gravity, the weird
  hunger of things for each other,
so strong it can take your legs right out from under you,
     send you back

  floundering for breath down the scarp
of shingle to where you came from, sun and earth and moon
     and water,
   everything needful.

4.

We're here the Tommies sang *because we're here because we're*
        here. And here
    tonight it's Dover
  where he steps down from the transport

        shivering,
    here where he started
  out, this stopgap town now turned in-
exorably home. He's back from the front, eyes bandaged,

    feeling the sea wind
  describe a familiar corner,
hearing his name called over the drawl of the shingle
        but seeing

  nothing – only that final blaze
of the shell he will never get out of his head now
        whatever
    he turns his hand to.

The war will be going on in his skull forever.
        He musters
    cramping limbs. He lights
  a cigarette, facing the sea.

5.

     We face it
    too now, you and I,
  father and son, the same fraught sea
preparing its ground with the same senseless precision,

    the same symmetry,
  we watch it rehearse the shoreline
over and over like a code imperfectly read,
    a lesson

  not yet learned by heart. Close your eyes:
you can hear the breakers at their immemorial
    handicraft,
   sifting, re-sifting,

as you might pick through spindrift of a life for salvage
    and pattern
   if any pattern
  could still be ours for the choosing,

    or the way
   a blind man's fingers
  fumble across a tabletop,
sorting rattan and wicker, laying them out to work.

John McAuliffe
The Rebuild

Walking upstairs into the dark –
they'd ripped out the electrics
to put in the new stairs –
she gripped where the banister had been

and tipped a little, like she'd taken a drink,
or lost a heel, or aged overnight by years,
but steadying herself, she went on
making another note of what they must fix

and entered the plasterboard attic
which emerged from the dark as bins, papers,
a toolbox, a bucket of water with a half pint of milk in,
all half-lit by the roof-opening velux

and the fancier wall-mounted window – black,
argon-filled – which she'd known,
as she signed the cheque, she'd paid too much for
and knew now, as she stepped around the nails and tacks

that dotted the dust-thick floor,
were doing no good at all, letting in
not only the noise of the last birds flying back
to the garden's rowans and lilacs

whose waving branches she could hear
swaying in the late evening's cool sonics –
familiar, quiet, unpredictable music
above the shattered old roof on the unmown lawn –

but also, farther off, a bus's creaking brakes
at the stop a street away, hearing even,
nothing in her hand, the doors clatter open and the driver
name the price, there and back.

Robyn Bolam
Winter Solstice at the High Voltage Laboratory

This big green metallic barn keeps fields in cages –
large ones we could run around in, but never do,
and some so small they sit on a bench with only
a hand entering carefully. At feeding time,
safely outside, keepers switch on the fields, record
how much has been consumed, what damage done, how long
it took. Electrons are excited, and charges,
hungry for volts, grow hot while parts snap or explode.

Now, a shed breaks down – heliotrope above, white
below – like a collapsing mushroom. An ion
engine starts to turn, wind park cables are stressed out,
plasmas used to propel us into space before
the Christmas shut-down. For the year, it's the darkest
day yet, but raw light fizzes in this bloodless zoo
as electric trees wink and insulated seas
flow over the coastline's high voltage silhouette.

Howard Wright
Artaud

God exists, but He will not give reason, wherefore
or cause why He should. Death is close and salvation far.

Suddenly my arm is numb from the shoulder down.
My writing arm, drinking arm, for a night on the town.

My paws are dead in their joints. My clenching paws,
my fists. My world is a lobster and comes with claws.

I raise my tingling arm and the numbness lingers
in my wrist, my palm, my soft white trigger-fingers.

The Flats

They have open skies up there under a quinine moon,
and suicide pesters the mind. The cratered face squints
into the space between office heaven and government hell,
the sky, its maker, following in a black limousine

through a tight city where no one will tell. Up there,
dreams stay the distance, a suitable miasma, and top-
of-the-range plasma jitters in Tretchikoff green.
Santa climbs the walls and windows are locked.

A strip of light then, like film unreeled at a ceiling bulb,
runs the height of the stairwell to the limits of solitude;
there, all the rooms are held together by tension
and dropped from an alien ship out of Wyndham or Wells,

stunted tower blocks stopped in their tracks from lumbering
across town and country by something in the air, something
rising from the earth. The open skies look down,
surround and threaten, and the height is a barricade.

Stephen McNeilly
Baron Samedi

I have seen him, watching,
prowling the balcony and pressing his

nose against the window. Once, on the high
street, he whispered "I shall put you in my

pocket". He was tall, a mad old man,
dressed in black, with a top hat.

Another time, he took residence in the cupboard
under the stairs. This was at Blake Avenue.

I was alone when suddenly I noticed the door of
the cupboard was open, and a horror

blinded me. I turned and ran. Just after that he
began to visit me every night in my bed.

It was a ritual. I had to sleep on my left side,
my face to the wall. I would wait, trembling all over,

and he would appear, a very conventional skeleton,
with a bow-tie and cigar, leaving a trail of blood.

I then had permission to turn on my right side,
he would go away and I could sleep in peace.

Liz Berry
Grasshopper Warbler

Amongst the iris beds at Dimmingsdale
all May I waited,
sat out on the bow each evening
as day fell into the arms of night
and searched the twilight for your voice,
unpicking the dusk-song – for what?
A cricket, a mill wheel,
a girl spinning straw in her lonely tower?
I scanned the reedclumps and the meadowsweet
for your skulking creep, shy mouse-bird
fossicking in your secret world.

How those weeks seemed endless,
waiting too for the little creature that grew inside me
unseen, unheard, unknowable as you
in his private dark.
I was always listening, never unafraid.
I made fool's bargains with the fields:
keep jack-in-the-hedge flowering in an egg cup
and he would live;
see a kit – yes; three magpies – yes;
hear you, your song, your grasshopper song
to feel him trembling through me
like the wind through the reeds.

Nights I fretted you would never come,
the rushes alive with everything but you,
the moon waning too quickly into June.
I was raw, heart-bare, a shorn cornfield, willow stripped,
until that gloaming, sweet gloaming, weeks on,
when I heard you calling in the cut's half-light,
reeling and insistent as that tiny heartbeart.
Small bird, amongst the irises
I knelt and I wept.

Scenes from *The Passion*: The First Path

When you found me there was nothing beautiful about me.
I wasn't even human
                  just a mongrel
kicked out into the snow on Maundy Thursday
when all the world was sorrow,
when old girls' hands were raw as they cracked
the ice on their birdbaths,
when the priest wept in Saint Jude the Apostle
as he knelt to wash the feet of an altar boy.

I was filth,
        running away from God knows what,
my haunches sore with bruises,
my spine knuckling the ruin of my coat.

Running through the town
                      away from the horses
who bowed their heads to the donkey-bite,
away from the boy in the bus shelter
                      who turned from me
to receive a snowflake
like a wafer on his tongue.
Lord help me
        I did things I would once
have been ashamed of.

Now no one would come near me,
                    they feared
the hunger that gnawed and whined in my bones,
the hurt I would carry into their houses.

Only you dared follow
                upon the track
of my bloodied paw prints in the ice,
where the trees held snow in their arms
like winding sheets.

                    You came for me there
                                close, low,
calling a name that was not mine.
Calling *wench, my wench*
as the tongues of the church bells rang mute.

At your scent on the air,
                    I shot
through the woods – a grey cry –
so raw only the dusk could touch me

but you were patient,
                    waited
through the dense muffled hours
until darkness dropped and I sank into the midden
behind the factory
and the chimneys cast a wreath of ash upon me.

                    You touched me then,
                when I was nothing but dirt,
took off your glove and laid your palm upon my throat,
slipped the loop of the rope,
                    lifted me
into your arms and carried me home
                                along the first path.

In the banks the foxes barked *alleluia alleluia*.

The blizzard tumbled upon us like confetti
and I, little bitch, blue bruise,
saw myself in your eyes:
                    a bride.

Scenes from *The Passion*: The Evening

There is an alley
where you can go,
where you can kiss
someone's mouth
until you climb
inside them, force
your way in, push
your cells into their cells
and became one
creature – angelic.
It isn't the way
you'd dream it.
There is piss,
dew damp moss crawling
across the brick.
Some nights it is so dark
you must enter only
by touch.
Walk by in the light
and it will seem
like nothing.
The scripture
is written by wenches:
4eva, L+J, I.T.A.L.Y.
A heart jagged in two.
But what you'll make there
it's not love,
it's not weighed
down with that,
it's feather, air,
an at-once exultation

of being not
of this time, this alley,
this shitty
good for no one,
shut-down town.
I never went there,
I promise you.
I never knew
such sweet violence.
Though there are mornings
now, miles from that place,
when I wake
with the thought of it:
wet and bitten, half-
winged.

Jack Underwood
Some Gods

God with eagle's head and five-pointed-star insignia on palms of hands; God connected to seven IV drips with fire coming out of mouth; God made of warts; God with horse's legs and head of ram reading names from a scroll pointing to a hole in the ground; God surrounded by representatives from the animal kingdom; God surrounded by representatives from the kingdom of global finance; God with cobbler's last and washing line with human faces pegged along; God with merciful expression holding knife and fork; God as a female infant; God with stomach as gumball machine; God as smiling coma patient between starchy cotton sheets surrounded by cards and flowers; God banging human skull-gavel to silence a courtroom of lesser gods; God being led into a courtroom and asked to confirm holy name; God in fool's attire inviting you to play a game of rummy; God as Bronze Medalist forcing smile on podium; God as golden ball of light forming in your chest; God as a feeling of intense and sudden cold; God as a feeling of sudden loneliness; God as a cup in your house that you haven't yet recognised as God but drink from nearly every day; God as a dead robin; God as the eye of a dead robin; God as your barely visible reflection in the eye of a dead robin.

Second

for Toby Underwood

If I lived in a cave and you were my only visitor,
what would I tell you that the walls had told me?
That people are unfinished and are made between
each other, that worry is either a Mexican finger trap
or the revolving door to a hospital foyer, that love
is a feeling deferred, which is why it weighs negative
and sucks on you like a cruise ship disappearing?

I would probably warn you to never feel mystical:
nothing is mystical. I would tell you to let yourself
be sad, if being sad is what happens when a person,
awkward in the universe as a plum on a plate,
doffs their day to the inaccessibility of other days,
and loosens their tie on the sofa to let some life out.

Spring

        is here so now the plants and animals
are starting to have sex again. We've unblocked
the drain of its crud and bumf, the smell is waning.
We've washed the gravel, and piled the fox turds
in a far off corner. We are wearing slightly fewer clothes.
Our bodies, newly exposed, are strangers to themselves.
They chime against the air. A thought arrives of our life
together, yet to come. It configures like a beam of dust.
Look, this plant has made it through the winter you say,
as millions of photons whoosh through my hands.

GALLERY Sylvia Plath Drawings

Ted Hughes, 1956. Pen and ink on paper, 21.5 x 14 cm.

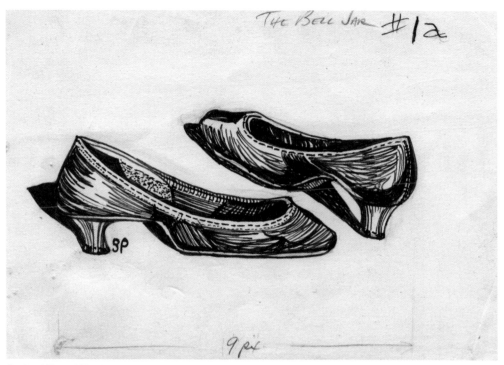

Study of Shoes, 1956. Pen and ink on paper, 10 x 14 cm (intended for use in *The Bell Jar*, 1963).

Sylvia Plath: Drawings assembles sketches the poet made between 1955 and 1957. During these years, while on a Fulbright Fellowship to Cambridge, she met Ted Hughes. They married in secret and went on honeymoon to Paris and Spain, before going to the US in June 1957. Plath sketched in pen and ink regularly at the time, often with Hughes at her side reading or writing. She described art as "her deepest source of inspiration" and was devoted to the work of "primitives like Henri Rousseau, Gauguin, Paul Klee, and De Chirico." She was excited by her own drawing and pleased with its development, as she wrote to her mother from Paris: "I feel I'm developing a kind of primitive style of my own".

The drawings are those Hughes gave to his children shortly before his death in October 1998. The book is introduced by Frieda Hughes, and it includes pertinent extracts from Plath's letters and from her journal.

Images from *Sylvia Plath Drawings*, with an introduction by Frieda Hughes, published by Faber, 2013, £16.99, ISBN 9780571295210. Drawings © The Estate of Sylvia Plath.

Wuthering Heights Today, 1956, near
Haworth, Yorkshire. Pen and ink on
paper, signed with initials, typed
with title, 11.2 x 19.8 cm

Willow near Grantchester.
Pencil, pen and ink on
paper, 21.5 x 14 cm

Diminishing Returns

CONOR O'CALLAGHAN

Matthew Francis, *Muscovy*, Faber, £12.99, ISBN 9780571297351;
Fleur Adcock, *Glass Wings*, Bloodaxe, £9.95, ISBN 9781852249731

There are some things that just never sound right: Irish wine, Cockney rappers, Julius Caesar in Barnsley... A poet of the Oulipian persuasion who is based in Wales might well fall into that category. Matthew Francis is a very good poet who deserves wider acclaim, a prize or two even. His fourth collection, *Muscovy*, continues his foray into the more fabular narratives of history's "long night". A man flies to the moon in a machine powered by geese. A shadowy Andrew Marvell sails/sleds his way to Moscow as a royal emissary. An emperor's concubine awaits the empress's vindictive whim. And so on.

I really enjoyed this book. Francis has clearly read widely, especially in Victoriana, and there is a heck of a lot of information here. These are substantial, ambitious poems fuelled by depth and dazzling syntactic energy. Francis shifts registers effortlessly, throws voices and generally whips the proverbial cast of thousands through his hoops with a ringmaster's aplomb. He has great feel for matter's sheen and light's texture, for the "soft / after-dark flashes without thunder" and the "spooklights of bog country". Metaphors come so thick and fast that his work can feel retro, positively Martian. There is even nostalgia to his Perec-inspired game-spinning, an old-school lyric beauty amid his symbols-in-lieu-of-letters codology:

> He~e the ~ive~
> un~ive~s itself,
> becomes estua~y
> and unp~onounceable.   ('Enigma Variations')

Why isn't Francis more celebrated? The more trite thesis would involve that Oulipian thing. You could argue that the work has a hollow core. Predictably, the lyric 'I' is at a premium and the vast majority of poems collected here involve researched narrative rather than personal experience. The lights are on, you could argue, are indeed blinding betimes, yet there is seldom anybody at home. But that's not right. Ultimately, nothing feels cold about Francis's work: his every image is incandescent and even that wackier stuff has oodles of charisma.

It may, more darkly, have something to do with his formal preoccupations and his ear for natural cadence. Almost every poem here is structured around an elaborate syllabic count of which even Dylan Thomas might have been proud. The title poem, for example, is built in 11-syllable units. The longer opener operates on a self-imposed law of diminishing returns both in stanzaic length and syllabic line. Once noticed, it becomes impossible to ignore. And it is impossible not to notice, not to approach fresh poems with a pencil and a ladder of numbers in the margins. Please read this aloud and see how it sounds:

> A bear would have more grace than these men who dance
> as if they no longer know where the ground is.   ('Muscovy')

Or try this:

> The barenecked poet launched a toy boat
> on the mountain streams, a cat on board
> with a face the same shape as his own.   ('Cwm Elan')

Make your own mind up. Perhaps this is some tanka/cynghanedd hybrid. To my ear, for all their brilliance, their visual pyrotechnics, too many lines get locked into similar stoned atonal monosyllables dictated by the chosen forms. There are too many moments when the poems are rhythmically inaccessible. It may be complete coincidence, but the most apparently personal poem here, 'Was', is also the most musical and beautiful:

> The TV was afloat on a sea of fuzz.
> It was switched on early to let it breathe.
> The end of it was a diminishing star.

Muscovy is a lovely book and, it needs saying, head-and-shoulders above most collections published anywhere this year. In those moments when Francis loosens his vice-like grip on structure, lets a little more of himself drift in and even permits his poems to hum to themselves occasionally, he becomes a very special poet indeed.

Fleur Adcock is one of those poets who has played, throughout her career, a deceptively dangerous game. Quite formal poems about family and ancestry, depending heavily on exquisite pinprick ironies and a tone described as "laconic" in every other review of her many books, is not obviously the stuff of danger. But laconism is a risky business and can fall badly flat in lesser hands. Adcock's finest books, *The Inner Harbour* or *Time Zones* perhaps, seem to thrive on this all-or-nothing high stakes/low style tension that a more demonstrative lyricism can easily fudge.

Glass Wings, her tenth original collection, is decidedly autumnal Fleur. Its impulse to elegise is to be expected of a poet in her eightieth year. The book is broken into four sections, each of which returns to the past and inheritance and mortality from different perspectives. We get a section addressing peers and the vagaries of aging; a suite of family occasions; yet more dim and distant ancestors, and a nice sequence in praise of insects.

At her best in *Glass Wings* Adcock can be funny and lusty and profound in a single image. "How can it be reprehensible?" she asks in defence of necrophilia. "The looks on their dead faces, as they plunge / into you...". As several of her strongest advocates have long since noted, Adcock's poetry is at its most powerful when actively battling the lure of freedom and excess. There remains fascination to her plain-spokenness, to her puritan almost-absolute resistance of metaphor's transubstantiation. "Here, I see," she writes at one point, "I should slip in a flattering metaphor." Needless to say, she doesn't. You could even argue that the whole book is preoccupied with metaphor, things becoming other things, "lives devoted to / being something else." Arguably the finest single passage occurs in the middle section of 'The Translator', where the poet momentarily translates herself into her ancestral subject:

> Being him:
> sifting through flakes and flecks
> of Hebrew; winnowing out
> seeds of meaning; choking
> on obscurities, the chaff
> of mistranscriptions, howlers,
> ambiguities, the never-before-seen.

Poets, alas, are rarely at their best when praising fellow poets in verse. F.R. Leavis glued together the final pages of Eliot's *Collected* to spare himself the blushes of Old Possum's homage to Walter de la Mare. The sentiments of those poems here in dedication to Michael Longley and Roy Fisher might have been better left to private letters. Even the elegy for Adcock's first husband, Alistair Campbell, is scarcely rescued by a closing echo of Catullus. Equally, most of those poems drawing upon family history feel like out-takes from *Looking Back*, Adcock's more successful collection of 1997. The trouble is, when that essential delicate tension loses tautness, seriously slackens off, we are left with likeable, rambling self-effacement in the former section:

> you know how tricky such commissions are –
> although you'd bring to them your customary
> elegance, intelligence and wit [...]
>
> ('An 80th Birthday Card for Roy')

and versified research in the latter:

> Twenty-three years later, the will
> of John Clayton of Syston, carpenter –
> half the length and more perfunctory,
> with all that he owns left to his wife [...] ('William Clayton, 1725')

If *Glass Wings* is your first encounter with the work of Fleur Adcock, a) for shame, and b) start elsewhere. Adcock is too good and too influential to deserve easy dismissal. But she is also too smart to be jollied along with faint praise. Though containing many familiar reminders of just how fine she can be, *Glass Wings* is unlikely to be remembered among her better books.

Conor O'Callaghan's *The Sun King* (2013) is published by Gallery Press.

B

P is for Photography, Puns, Paris

JUDY BROWN

Sinéad Morrissey, *Parallax*, Carcanet, £9.95, ISBN 9781847772046;
Ahren Warner, *Pretty*, Bloodaxe, £9.95, ISBN 9781852249779

There's an engineered exactness to Sinéad Morrissey's fifth collection, with its carefully laid trail of thematic markers. The poems flick and twist round ideas of mutability, and the unreliability of vision, photos, TV and film. The fragile shimmer of what little can be safeguarded in moving and unmoving pictures contrasts with the control these careful, formal poems exert over their material.

The title's definition stresses the importance of where you're looking from, but the poems show us a disorientating range of representations skewed for many reasons. Two poems touch on deliberate alteration – of photographs in 'The Doctors', and, more tangentially in 'Shadows', of textbooks. Distortions of sight may have medical causes: 'Migraine' describes the visual "unpick[ings]" which prefigure an attack. Colour may shift to black-and-white, and back; a shadow could be "blood in a black-and-white video".

Television or film often forms a backdrop to events as well as being a source of imagery in poems on other topics (such as "the white dot of the television" in 'Home Birth'). 'The Evil Key' muses on the theme tunes to Scandinavian detective series. Other poems talk directly of the nature of photography, whilst 'The Mutoscope' is a form of primitive film made of photographs: "It lasts a minute, their having-been-written onto light". A key poem is the lovely 'Photographing Lowry's House' in which a photographer goes to Lowry's home after his death. As it is being dismantled, he photographs what he can in the permitted half hour: "without a flash / the staircase seeming flounced / in the train of a bridal dress, / shimmery". Although he is conservator, not despoiler, the removal is so swift, it is:

> [...] as though I stood in Lascaux
> among its sprinting fawns

and my very breath
was wrecking what I stared at.

In the end, part of what holds him is emptiness itself: ocean canvases, "de-peopled", the sea "over and over"; trilby and mac, hanging.

The thematic patterning is surprisingly insistent, so it's impressive how varied the poems feel, and how precisely they achieve their friable effects, like the "fractured signalling" of 'Lighthouse'. The formal and syntactical control is resolute. The one-sentence 'Baltimore' skilfully evokes a mother's endless listening for her child's crying, where even "the white space / between radio stations when no voice / comes at all and the crackling static / might be swallowing whole a child's / small call for help". Indeed, silence itself may "envelop [...] / a ghost cry, one I've made up". The poem is full of noises cancelling each other out, only to end with "the air / of the landing thick with something missed", now that the child is asleep.

Frailty of visual records is balanced with physical frailty – gruesome TV murders, the deaths that accompany birth and "viruses [which] churned out / relaxed, unkillable replicas of themselves" ('Last Winter'). 'V is for Veteran' moves at speed from a child's spelling book to an image of horror and pity invading a home. Even in poems not concerned with family life, children appear on the periphery or in metaphor, vulnerable.

There's a wide range of verse forms and Morrissey excels in both long and short lines. Whilst the terse lyrics dazzle in a tiny space, the collection is anchored with long poems which handle their expansiveness with panache – particularly 'Photographing Lowry's House' and 'A Matter of Life and Death'. Arguably, her skill may very occasionally allow a poem to stretch out a little longer than seems strictly necessary: if so, one never minds.

One of the excitements of Ahren Warner's *Pretty* is how sound drives the construction of his poems, creating a distinctive, allusive architecture. The opening sequence 'Lutèce, te amo' has a poem for each of Paris's 20 arrondissements. Other poets might have done that, but probably wouldn't have used, as another structural element, the stitching through the poems of derivatives of three 'seed' words (*désinvolte*, *envolver* and *involvere*, from French, Spanish and Latin respectively) relating to being 'unbuttoned' or casual, or to covering or wrapping up. In addition to the holding pattern of rhyme in many poems, the joy of etymological connection, homophone or near-homophone, repeat and pun (often across languages), can create the pivot point for a transition within an individual poem, or the satisfaction for a close. This cityscape of poems rarely sounds less than gorgeous.

The sequence is a wander as much among concepts, words and history as amongst the buildings and characters of Paris. Warner seems as at home with this barrow of cultural artefacts as the speaker and his companion have become with Paris, "now our home, our homely *involvendum*... the Tour Eiffel no longer notable, no longer noticed" ('XVII This'). 'Lutèce, te amo' is studded with names – places, cheeses, the cast list of history. Names are a common trick in contemporary poetry, but Warner is doing something entirely individual, far more to do with sound and widening the screen, than the usual stab at specificity and grounding. French words naturally affect tone, but the deliberately self-aware references are integral to each poem's musical as well as connotative character. En masse, too, the often polysllyabic French names create a pervasive music which threads through and under the variant tunes.

Several poems in this sequence have prepositions or conjunctions as titles, and relation and placement are crucial to this work. Warner's range of diction is astounding and refreshingly bold, from Greek prosodic terms to the scabrous, Sartre's "philosopher-cum", the daft play of arsis, arse (and *ars*). That's partly it – the bright electricity of disjunction – and how these things all cohere. The prepositions of the Parisian sequence link past and present, horror and beauty, low and high, in a series of energetic juxtapositions. And all the while the poems show themselves thinking, making connections. The resulting mixture is what makes a home, as 'XVII This' acknowledges.

Warner is too sophisticated not to use a simple construction where it works. Several of my favourite poems in the sequence unfold on syntactical recipes using repetition ('XVIII Before' or 'XX Having'). Similarly, the list of colours making up "a kaleidoscope of red" in the poem 'after' Bacon's Vélazquez-inspired painting is stunningly effective.

A later sequence, '*Metousiois*', is a powerful presence, its title referring to a concept close to transubstantiation. Frightening physical mutability has already been glimpsed in 'Lutèce', but here flesh and bodies come to the fore – sometimes ugly, decaying, unhomely ("a waxed rind, / a terrine of silt and scud"). At other times the speaker takes comfort in moving his fingers across his own body:

> tracing the contours of my self – near catatonic –
> [...]
> where, beneath the glaze of *cogitans*, touch
> can trigger surety – flesh and bone assurance...

With no principle of order, "carrion insists, exists as affirmation", but in the last poem of the sequence the critical perusal of the body is interrupted and then transformed in sex – "*this*, our sweat-glazed *metousiosis*." The mesmeric and feverish abstractions of the closing 'Nervometer' sequence, based on Antonin Artaud's work, feel almost austere in texture by contrast.

Pretty is a witty and knowing collection, and aptly titled, since these are praise poems – to cities, homes, to the body's glory and decay, to the concepts and sounds that words hold and release.

Judy Brown's first collection, *Loudness* (Seren), was shortlisted for the 2011 Forward Prize for Best First Collection. She is Poet-in-Residence at the Wordsworth Trust.

ℬ

Master of the Singing Line

STEPHEN ROMER

Robert Graves, *Selected Poems*, ed. Michael Longley,
Faber, £15.99, ISBN 9780571283835

In his engaging introduction to this volume, Michael Longley recalls how he and his comrade at Trinity College Dublin, Derek Mahon, "inhaled poetry with our Sweet Afton cigarettes". To these tyros, Robert Graves emerged as a hero, chiefly as a "master of the singing line". Memorability is a hallmark of Graves's poetry, and Longley's instinct, to gather first the poems thus remembered over the years – they form "the heartbeat" of the selection – is surely sound. My own favourites, 'Love Without Hope', 'Pure Death', 'Mid-Winter Waking', 'Never Such love', 'A Last Poem' among them, are all in. Some of these, Longley states fair and square, "will last as long as the language". Miranda Seymour, who wrote Graves's biography, the hugely enjoyable *Life On the Edge* (1995), opens with an eye-catching phrase: "In twentieth-century poetry, Robert Graves is to love what Philip Larkin is to mortality", and it is as a love poet – albeit one of a strangely dogmatic type – that he wanted to be remembered. To Malcolm Muggeridge's impertinent question in a 1965 BBC interview, as to why he wrote so much about "love and women", Graves replied nonchalantly "that's what poetry's mostly about, isn't it?" But Longley's selection tilts the conventional view in another direction: his mission is to rescue Graves as a war poet, one who belongs with Owen and Sassoon. Graves served with the latter in the Royal Welch Fusiliers, and as a victim of shell-shock was with both poets under the supervision of the great doctor William Rivers at Craiglockhart – "a momentous coincidence of talent, with Graves a crucial part of it", as Longley says. In his successive *Collected*s, Graves himself came to exclude nearly all his war poetry, and the reasons are various. On one occasion he explained that "they were too obviously written in the war-poetry boom". By 1918, in fact, he already announced to Sassoon that "worrying about the War is no longer a sacred duty with me".

Graves wrote some memorable, and some quirky, war poems. They do not, however, constitute a univocal voice of protest, as the combined, formidable work of Owen and Sassoon undoubtedly does. This may be another reason for their suppression. What they do chiefly constitute is a memorial to the deep friendships, sometimes shading into the homoerotic – the "beautiful comrade-looks" – that bound the men in the trenches. The memorial poem to David Thomas, to whom both Graves and Sassoon were devoted, 'Not Dead', begins "Walking through trees to cool my heat and pain, / I know that David's with me here again", and ends wonderfully:

> All that is simple, happy, strong, he is.
> Over the whole wood in a little while
> Breaks his slow smile.

Longley is surely right when he suggests that the war poems "are love poems in their way". Other pieces include 'A Dead Boche', which is a verbal description to set alongside a Dix etching: "Big-bellied, spectacled, crop-haired, / Dribbling black blood from nose and beard". Longley has salvaged a sprightly 'Blighty' poem, 'Return', in the ballad-like metre Graves could use so well:

> But cushy wounds don't last a man too long,
> And now, poor lad, he sings this bitter song:
> 'Back to La Bassée, to the same old hell,
> Givenchy, Cuinchey, Cambrin, Loos, Vermelles.'

Also included is the remarkable 'Letter from Wales', a searching, metaphysically fraught poem addressed to Sassoon, written in 1925, and concerning the moment when Graves was mistakenly reported killed, and

Sassoon was already beginning an elegy for him. After such experience, and such close brushes with death, Graves asks urgently, "Who are we?"

It was in fact his survival at the Somme, where so many of his comrades died, that instilled in Graves something like a sacred mission – he would become a *musarum sacerdos*, his life dedicated to serving the muse. After his marriage to Nancy Nicholson broke down, precipitated by the meeting with Laura Riding in 1926, the sheer force of whose personality and intellect was to fascinate and subjugate Graves for 13 years, serving the muse became a lived reality. Graves is *polumetis* – myriad minded – and in the Majorcan years that followed he produced poems, novels (including the 'Claudius' series), scenarios, social history and, in collaboration with Riding's incisive, severe intellect, brilliant criticism, as in the study *Modernist Poetry*. When they first became lovers he wrote 'Pure Death', which opens with absolute authority:

> We looked, we loved, and therewith instantly
> Death became terrible to you and me.

There is no question that life alongside the charismatic Riding, with its puritanical work ethic – she soon put a ban on sex – brought great intellectual rewards and fed into the conception of *The White Goddess*, Graves's inimitable "grammar of poetic myth" that was published in 1948, nearly ten years after the couple had broken up. There was witchery, a potential for moral evil in Riding, although she was overtly intent on moral 'purity' (she invented a protocol for Literal Morality) and on single-handedly (with her acolytes) averting the coming of war. Graves surely recognised her dark side, but he remained voluntarily in thrall. "If strange things happen where she is", he writes in 'On Portents'

> Such portents are not to be wondered at,
> Being tourbillions in Time made
> By the strong pulling of her bladed mind
> Through that ever-reluctant element.

That quatrain shows Graves at his sophisticated best – the thought complex but the imagery clear and the music tough and subtle.

After *The White Goddess*, Graves came to define himself formally as a muse poet: "A Muse-poet falls in love, absolutely, and his true love is for him the embodiment of the Muse". He meant this seriously, believing in the primacy of the goddess in a primitive matriarchal religion. "There is one story and one story only", he says in the poem to his youngest son 'To Juan at the Winter Solstice'. In prefaces and public lectures he came increasingly to make disarming and defiant statements like "My main theme was always the practical impossibility, transcended only by a belief in miracle, of absolute love continuing between man and woman." Only moon-inspired Muse poetry was the genuine article, not the poems of Apollonian technique, though it must be said that Graves's classical metric and his eschewing of Modernist techniques like ellipsis and parataxis has something always of Apollonian measure. To abandon this traditional resource, or to "jazz up" his poetry in Modernist vein (the expression is his), would be for one of his temperament – he seems to know – perilous. "There's a cool web of language winds us in," he writes in one of his most famous poems, and "if we let our tongues lose self-possession [...] We shall go mad no doubt and die that way".

Graves remained true to the "singing line". He remained more in the camp of "clarity", of Hardy or Frost, than with Pound or Eliot, though he could at times be as grandly eloquent as his fellow Irishman, Yeats. His public denunciations of the High Modernists were notorious – even as great a poet as David Jones, who worked in some of the same areas as Graves – was dismissed as a plagiarist! Longley follows most editors in cutting down the increasingly debile "muse poetry" of the last phase – inspired by four younger women, who in turn "embodied" the goddess for Graves, during the allotted time span of three to four years. I have some sympathy with "muse poetry"; it can be the necessary fuel, though the fact that these forays into romantic ecstasy and agony were made from the security of his marriage to Beryl, who apparently tolerated them, makes the whole business irksome. Beryl, in fact, inspired finer poems, at the beginning of their marriage, none more so than the exquisite 'Mid-Winter Waking':

> Be witness that on waking, this mid-winter,
> I found her hand in mine laid closely
> Who shall watch out the Spring with me.
> We stared in silence all around us
> But found no winter anywhere to see.

This has none of the trappings of the "goddess" about it – just a spontaneous, beautifully cadenced record of something like deep joy recovered.

Stephen Romer's translation of *The Arrière-pays* by Yves Bonnefoy (Seagull Books) was published in 2012 and his *French Decadent Tales* (Oxford World's Classics) in May this year.

The Wings and Claws

SAM RIVIERE

Christopher Reid, *Six Bad Poets*, Faber, £12.99, ISBN 9780571304035

Christopher Reid's best books generally exceed the standard collection's assortment of poems united by virtue of being produced over the same five or six years. *A Scattering* (2009) was an original and intense treatment of grief; most of 2012's *Nonsense* was an ambitious, vivid and affecting narrative poem called 'Professor Winterthorn's Journey'; his earlier act of ventriloquism, *Katerina Brac*, was first published as the translation of a (fictional, it turned out) female Eastern European poet. While the title of *Six Bad Poets* suggests further identity games might be afoot (reminiscent perhaps of Kenneth Koch's *Some South American Poets*), the collection finds Reid again in his scaled-up narrative mode. It is a lighter, more whimsical undertaking than his last long poem, but more tightly and intricately structured. You get the impression Reid had a lot of fun writing this, and it's probably fair to say that the extent to which "a satire of London literary life" appeals to you will determine how much you'll enjoy the book.

Billed as a "farce-in-verse", *Six Bad Poets* introduces its eponymous characters in single file – three men, three women, four of them middle-aged to old, two fairly young – in neat sections of six six-line stanzas, each comfortably occupying a double-spread. Six of these sections make up a chapter, of which there are six. I dread a sestina as much as the next person, but there is something undeniably satisfying and sestina-like about how the book rolls out in this swift and cyclical way. Each section concerns itself with one poet, and the poet that ends a section begins the next. This is replicated at the level of line as well, with dextrous rhymes and half-rhymes connecting the beginnings and ends of each stanza. Whether or not you get the same pleasure out of this sort of echoing structural play as I do, it indicates the high levels of patterning and wiring that have gone into mapping out and executing the poem.

The plot is as linked-up and overlapping as the formal structure that contains it. To begin with, Charles Prime, poet and 77-year-old vulture, is back in London after a decade in prison for an undisclosed crime. He hangs around at funerals he hasn't been invited to and is gradually restored to the scene of which he was once the centre. Among the first he latches onto are Antonia Candling and Bryony Butters, poets and warring friends whose barbed relationship of mutual sympathy and ruthless competition is one of the book's highlights:

> Bryony Butters, poet, novelist, and more besides,
> has rung Antonia Candling, her friend, to tell her
> that she, Bryony, has been commissioned to edit
> a major new poetry anthology.
> It's early in the morning and she knows
> Antonia will be jealous.

It's that wry detail, "early in the morning", that is typical of Reid, a choice which laces the neutral relaying of events with humour, while the repeated use of full names allows him to scold the vanities and envies of the poetry world with the wit and drama they frankly deserve. The story proceeds to entangle its other characters in the same way its language of sly rhyming works – associatively, by connection and coincidence – as to varying degrees they are snared in a plot that sees Prime, the Soho scavenger, gradually become the quarry. It would take too long to explain more here, which credits Reid's achievement of covering as much as he does in lines that never feel overpacked. Much of what occurs occurs off-screen, as it were (though you can imagine the book translating to TV as successfully as *The Song of Lunch*), and reaches the reader by filtering through the different characters like gossip – appropriately, some later dramatic episodes remain hazy, their details conflicted or indistinct, similar to the chains of hearsay any literary scene thrives on. Perhaps here, alongside the social inventions of rumour and elaboration, are the roots of literature as we know it.

The book really only falters in its depiction of the two younger poets. Jonathan Wilderness, a pony-tailed creature straight out of an early Martin Amis novel, has had no real-life counterpart since the end of the 1970s, and is a baffling anachronism when you consider the wealth of contemporary candidates for the part of misguided rock-and-roll poet (I would have bought a watered-down Pete Doherty, for instance). But least convincing is Dickensian waif Jane Streep, whose downward arc seems at best ill-informed and at worst to lean on assumptions that fail to correspond to reality so completely you can't even excuse them for being outdated. She is introduced as "a poet still in search of her voice", which underlines much of what doesn't work here: Streep feels pieced-together, convenient, almost without agency, and reminds me of the tendency of some novelists of Reid's generation to produce female characters whose only apparent purpose is to connect the male ones. Jane studied English, carries a basket bag, works in a kebab shop, sleeps with her lecturer and becomes a stripper. It's not to say that with the proper consideration a believable personality couldn't be found among these co-ordinates – the problem is the total haphazardness with which they've been selected as characterising shorthand, a series of plot points the character is shunted through, resulting in a kind of fantasy of a young woman's life which is so far off that its origins are actually a mystery. Other lapses include 'Kurdish Dave', and the general lack of technology: when you think of how fluidly other similarly orientated tales (*Tamara Drew*, for example) have incorporated phones and texts to assist their developments and twists, it seems like a missed opportunity here. Or just a conspicuous absence: Jane uses an *A to Z* rather than her phone to find a reading, and when at one point we encounter a "memory stick" I was left genuinely unsure if it wasn't some sort of tribal artefact employed by one character to assist her writing process. As registering a basic believability is important for the objectives of this book, it is hard to overlook some of this stuff. But it shouldn't and doesn't outweigh its strengths and sheer exuberance.

The imagistic touches that anchor Reid's narratives are among the most consistent pleasures of his writing: moments of stillness where a meaning rests. Derek Dufton is an academic and frustrated poet, slightly out on his own plot-wise (perhaps appropriately if he is what he seems to be, a dig at the British avant-garde), who makes an unsuccessful pass at a student. She bolts, and "He sits, feeling sick, while on his desk two coffees, / almost touching, grow cold." The acutely observed comedy of mistiming and misjudgement tips into tragedy in places, and gives *Six Bad Poets* the breadth – the "wings and claws" as Nabokov put it – of a novelistic space, which many actual novels twice its length often fail to open up.

Much of the action takes place in "deepest Fitzrovia"; London is always in the poem's lens, and in some ways emerges as the book's hidden subject. I'm not sure I've read anything that summons these parts of the city, their street-names inviting the scope of literary history, quite as completely and immediately as Reid does, partly because, as with the gatherings it describes, it is always the setting and hardly ever directly seen. Yet its unmistakable atmosphere is triggered throughout: the "light-shy pubs", the street-ends swinging past the bus window. London here is the home of the chance meeting, the missed stop, the spilled drink, the long lunch – perhaps the only theatre where the vying fortunes and reckless ambitions of these characters could retain the harsh comedy and mythological darkness at their edges and centres.

Sam Riviere's *81 Austerities* (Faber, 2012) won the Forward Prize for Best First Collection.

ℬ

Hendrix on Guitar, Handel on Harpsichord

KATHRYN GRAY

Caroline Bird, *The Hat-Stand Union*, Carcanet, £9.95, ISBN 9781847771643; John Agard, *Travel Light Travel Dark*, Bloodaxe, £9.95, ISBN 9781852249915; Sharon Morris, *Gospel Oak*, Enitharmon, £9.99, ISBN 9781907587238

R eaders of Caroline Bird's previous collections will be familiar with her particular brand of smart surrealism – the incongruity of the mundane set against frequently staggering leaps of invention. In her fourth offering, *The Hat-Stand Union*, she undoubtedly takes her ingenuity to new heights. There's much to intrigue between these pages. In 'Method Acting', a monomaniacal failed actress is stuck in the groove of Nina from *The Seagull* – a Chekhovian soul navigating the landscape and detritus of the everyday in pubs, Virgin Trains, chemists, multiplexes, and supermarkets, declaiming, and doomed by, the great master's miscommunications:

> There was no lake to wander by
> so I drifted about by the fish counter in Tesco.
> 'Am I much changed?' I asked the woman.
> She could not reply. 'You hair-net
> is the most melancholy thing I've seen,' I said.
> I meant it as a compliment. I was asked to leave.

'Mystery Tears' is the record of a once-vogue drug, inviting clever comparison with Ecstasy. In Bird's world, however, MDMA is turned on its head – with users scoring a drug which reduces them to lachrymose fits and isolation. It ruefully catalogues the decline of a relationship and how the narrator's partner "sadly became addicted to Mystery Tears / [...]/ 'It's so romantic,' she said, 'and yet I feel nothing.'" The 'high' becomes, in fact, the dissonance between display and authentic human feeling: "A dealer sold her stuff cut with / Fairy Liquid, street-name: River of Sorrow. / Our flat shook and dampened. I never / touched it. Each day she woke up / calmer and calmer."

The Hat-Stand Union presents a chilling ambiguity, exploring matters of subjectivity, art and life. Are Bird's creations themselves truly caught in these extraordinary worlds – or are their worlds merely projections of psychic breaks within the narrator? In 'Damage', for example, a dark, potted biography of a troubled woman with an unhappy end opens: "Her teddy bear eloped with her mother. / Her father went to buy flowers for himself / on Father's Day and never came home. Her grandma / was a waste-paper basket. She was raised by staplers."

Coming in at 93 pages, *The Hat-Stand Union* might have benefited from some winnowing, with 'A Dialogue Between Author and Muse', 'Hey Las Vegas', 'Prologue', and the ill-judged '9 Possible Reasons for Throwing a Cat into a Wheelie Bin' being, to my mind, just four instances of material which is clearly surplus to requirements, by comparison with material of a higher order elsewhere.

There is also a key problem with Bird's approach. Driven, as her poems are, by flights of fancy delivered by a uniformly wry voice, the element of reader-surprise is depleted. The extraordinary, when overly depended upon to achieve effect, becomes, like everything else, ultimately commonplace – even as one is sometimes scratching one's head to make sense of some of Bird's more arcane leaps. I began to wonder how much Bird has come to depend upon her own very evident facility, perhaps unnecessarily wary of the pleasures in directness. But, here and there, her quest to reach for oddity gives way instead to something that, for this reader, is welcome and satisfying. 'The Dry Well' and 'Corine', for example, are small, affecting lyrics – the restless Bird looks you straight in the eye, and these moments modulate the collection.

John Agard's *Travel Light Travel Dark* contains some bravura pieces and relates throughout an array of historical and cultural connections, all commendably lightly worn. One particular fact, new – and startling – to me: Congolese boys were brought to Llandudno, North Wales, in the late nineteenth century, to be skilled, and trained in Christian values, before returning home to spread the Gospel. Some never made it back and now lie buried in the Old Colwyn cemetery. Agard poignantly charts their distance in death from their native land: "As far as antelope's leap / from a pastor's last breath in a Colwyn workhouse / As far as born-laughing-Mwindo's floating drum / from the Amens of Congo's sons under Welsh ground" ('Congo to Llandudno'). Another, familiar connection: Hendrix and Handel, whose respective homes at 23 and 25 Brook Street are now merged into one, as the Handel House Museum. Agard merrily imagines the mother of all jam sessions across time: "Strange how the centuries evaporate / when transatlantic ghosts become housemates / and summer 1723 puts on the swinging sixties. // Hendrix on guitar. Handel on harpsichord" ('Jimi Hendrix and Handel Under One Roof'). Whimsy, of course – but it's no less enjoyable for that.

Two especially witty cricket poems in this collection stand out. 'Give the Ball to the Poet' is a great metaphor if ever there was one:

> Is all right when words sing
> in lyrical flight,
> but when dey also have grit
> and double bite,
> de literary boys dem call it
> ambiguity of meaning.
> I rather call it double entendre swing
> of a Michael Holding.

Meanwhile 'Prospero Caliban Cricket' makes for one unmissable test:

> Is cricket is cricket in yuh ricketics
> But from far it look like politics.
> Prospero wishing
> Shakespeare was de umpire,
> Caliban seeing a red ball
> and he see fire
> rising with glorious uncertainty.
> Prospero front pad forward with diplomacy

Travel Light Travel Dark includes lines so perfectly wrought they seemed as if they had always existed: "For an ocean knows the meaning of freedom / as water knows the reason for a bridge" ('Atlantic Libation').

And here's 'Enlightenment' in its entirety: "Before Newton's boyhood pebble / revealed to him its inward lesson / of truth's undiscovered ocean – / some dreaming soul branded savage / once stood on some uncharted shore / and heard the voice of thunder in a stone."

Only rarely does Agard miss his mark. The opening section, 'Colour Poems', for example, feels, cumulatively, too much like an exercise. And, occasionally, he's rather too neat, with a poem such as 'Starting Somewhere', in its calls for universal clemency, dodging exploration in favour of worthiness. A portrait of 'The Executioner' ("At the end of the day he returns / to his passion for roses / and garlands his wife's neck / with a rosary of kisses") is too reassuringly simplistic to be remotely credible. Evil may very well be banal. But it's never without its own innate complexity.

Despite this, Agard's collection is ambitious, various, ultimately winning – and its rhythms and textures offer something for the reader to truly savour.

Sharon Morris's *Gospel Oak* is a narrative of mutability and loss, landscape and peoples, time and record, endurance and evolution. It's a promising book, infused with the wonders of the natural world, most particularly the delights of Hampstead Heath – but with pleasures too often interrupted by over-exposition and intervention on the part of the poet. There is often simply too much telling and Morris seems reluctant to trust in the fidelity of image to convey meaning. 'Parliament Hill', for example, informs us that this is a "day, drear / that could sap all will; / no wind for flying kites, the city, / like expectation itself, / subjugated / under low grey cloud." Strike out four of those lines and the same significance will be understood. There's a problem of frequent overwriting and abstraction, too: "taproots strike / veridical / into the hiemal earth, / that deep / blue lake: / not yet the cessation / of things" ('Trees in Winter'); "Then / I will lose those adamantine doubts..." ('Zenith'); "the kind of beauty / that comes with light / as an assertion of will / in a time of apathy / and futility" ('Constable's View'). This is a shame, because when Morris achieves the clarity and concision of the striking image, she proves her skill. Drovers' cattle are "a horned contusion" ('Drovers' Roads'); days-old snow is rendered as "dirty rags" ('Galanthus Nivalis'); a hollow oak "stands / stag-headed / crimson" ('Veteran'). And Morris can, in deceptive simplicity, achieve transcendence: "Look further into the grain of things. / Listen to the silence" ('Again the Fall'). Laudable advice, there – for all of us.

Kathryn Gray's The Never-Never (Seren, 2004) was shortlisted for the Forward Prize for Best First Collection and the T.S. Eliot Prize.

Less Gross than Bodily

GREGORY LEADBETTER

Fred D'Aguiar, *The Rose of Toulouse*, Carcanet, £9.95, ISBN 9781847772299;
Leanne O'Sullivan, *The Mining Road*, Bloodaxe, £8.95, ISBN 9781852249687;
Marianne Burton, *She Inserts the Key*, Seren, £8.99, ISBN 9781781720387

T*he Rose of Toulouse* presents new perspectives on the political concerns that characterise Fred D'Aguiar's earlier work, with poems that feature the poet's own fugitive sense of self as lens, subject and scrutineer. Alongside the humane moral certitude that – while never resorting to bland assertion – D'Aguiar builds into his verse, there are doubts that unpick the seams of the political persona, as in the title poem: "I do not know what I want; / I do not want what I know". There is a palpable desire to be free from the legacies of human suffering, as in 'Calypso History Lesson', where "each day starts without the curse of history" – and often anger boils away to the plaintiveness of wish, where the half-transforming imagination lives what it cannot change: "I wish those tall ships at Africa's shore / Had dropped anchor to plant crops there", begins one such poem, with "No Atlantic road of bones from people / Dumped into the sea to form a wake".

This sense of tension and search for release is made more poignant by the consciousness of ageing that runs through the collection. Transitions through time feature as strongly here as transitions through postcolonial space. Finding their way beyond a straightforward lament for the slippage of the past from the grasp of the present, D'Aguiar's poems fasten upon more unexpected effects – how the past takes over, finds openings through which to pour and displace the present, as in 'Shoes My Father Wore':

> His shoes on my feet become my shoes
> on his feet. My feet take on his,
>
> transplanted on my body,
> his heels click and I dance.

The observing eye, itself saturated with memory, struggles for autonomy. Again, the personal finds an echo in the historical perspective.

'Legal Tender' treats the ambivalence of the 'freedom' won in the years following the abolition of slavery, in seeing

> Not a freed slave
> But the heads
> Of our parents
>
> Planted on the
> Round shoulders
> Of our children

Two particularly moving poems address the diagnosis of multiple sclerosis in the poet's own son. 'Wednesday's Child' begins with the morning sun, poised "to run my day, disguised as me, / My best and brightest side", before an email delivers the news, "And there I am, nothing... And fall, out of time", back into the memory of teaching his son how to ride a bike. Here memory begins the spontaneous task of healing – and consolation, of a kind, comes in the act of finding the right words to face it.

If I were to name the salient motive at the heart of this book, it would be that of finding strength in conditions that have no easy categories to fall back on – summed up, metaphorically, in the "longing for a country not on any map" at the cold junction of modern passport control ('Excise'). The long poem that concludes the collection, 'The Giant of Land's End', offers – in urban fairytale fashion – a vision of a situated self, hinted at throughout the collection. There is a craving for a post-historical statelessness, for a consciousness freshened by its own elemental pre-history: "Thrilled to be lost at last in things outside of myself / Until I belong to a world that ignores my footprint" ('Saturday, Ocean Creek'), or

> flying without benefit
> of wings or a passport, moving freely
> between places and no name strong
> enough to stick to my skin, except sea,
> sun, air, and the minerals in all three.   ('English')

The opening poem of *The Mining Road*, Leanne O'Sullivan's third collection, begins with "A hankering in the skull", and ends on the word "listening": between the two we have a tale about looking for a ghost ('Townland'). Taken together – hankering, listening, looking for something that might not be there – that atmospheric charge is a figure for the collection as a whole. O'Sullivan's voice is assured in its own gentleness. Her language laps softly at the reading mind – and uses that quality to penetrate further than less subtle methods might achieve. More often than not, her subject is "Something seen clearly when seen askew / like a boat glimpsed lightly on the mist" ('Vincit Qui Se Vincit') – a form of seeing that finds its way into the fabric of the language itself, as in the use of the word "on" in the lines just quoted: lifting the boat out of its literal element and into imaginative life.

Her poems often condense upon something sensed but which cannot be grasped or fixed, like the cold hand of the air: "the wind lining the sky / with unutterable thoughts" ('The Lights of New York'). Dreams are folded within dreams – as in the title poem: "my mother dreams her mother on the road... I dream them now together" – or 'Song', a beautifully achieved, quietly rhyming piece, again charged with the act of listening:

> As if through a gap in the floorboards
> of a dream I would make out her footfall
> hourly on the stairs, and afterwards
> a stillness on the landing, her breath small
> and hungry for my own small breathing.

O'Sullivan's sounds and images can creep up on the reader, with an innocence of approach that might be suddenly offset by a shift in the light. The steely and excellent 'Safe House' is a fine example of this – its darkly ironic title smuggling through a piercing study in Irish historical-political psychology.

The ethereal and elusive are similarly counter-poised throughout by an authoritative sensuousness, as in the love poems included here, and the folk-ish edge of a home-sage voice that captures the sense of threat – present or historical – to which it responds. These alluring qualities combine to make O'Sullivan's poetry at once both "lightening" and "darkening" in its effects – two words that, tellingly, recur throughout this collection.

Marianne Burton's *She Inserts the Key* was shortlisted for the Forward Prize for Best First Collection 2013 – and would have been a deserving winner. It is filled with night-spaces, death-spaces, and takes on the task of speaking there. "As with newborns, / eloquence fails", she writes, in one such meditation ('11am: Hallaton: Burial of the Dead') – but Burton's eloquence thrives at these margins. Flowers "seed in the mulch of our dead": "If one is picked, another drinks its sun. // Their darkness is not our darkness" ('The Flowers').

Her poetry is at once capable of metaphysical reach and domestic veracity. Wry acknowledgements of "the one uncluttered surface in the house" ('The Elephant-Headed God') blend with apprehensions akin to weather-sense: "in the owl-stirred blackness – / moon in the birdbath, wind in the grass – / something is getting up, filing its iron nails" ('Midnight: Hallaton: Before the Storm'). These poems are unafraid of unsettling thoughts – as when her sympathy with calves waiting to be taken to Melton market blends with the sound of "my daughter's tread, / padding in the dark from her bed / to mine. Veal-pink and cloven" ('The Devil's Cut'). The poems are bracing and direct, unflinching:

> Mother, all our lives are wasted.
> Look, my poor childish words
> have already outlived you.
>
> She does not know she is dead yet,
> has entered the place where she began,
> the usual unexpected human state of non-being.
>
> ('4am: Kitchen Table, East Ewell')

This authenticity of voice – an honesty, if only to the poem – earns the reader's trust, as well as attention. A dark-edged humour discloses itself throughout the collection, fending off any hint of excessive earnestness, bringing its mixed and nervous relief – as in 'I know I've already said goodbye', a version of Du Fu: "yesterday we serenaded the moon, we kissed, / We hugged. We always get on when we're pissed".

Burton's deftness and economy of image and diction are authoritative in their discipline and tact. Examples abound, but these lines glisten with such qualities:

> the river gleamed
> and lied about its purity, its noise
> lost under traffic as it hugged the dank
> places, dens of tears and tight lacing, rough
> sleep, soiled bodies, and the three a.m. leap.
>
> ('5am: London: I have held conversations')

She Inserts the Key is cosmopolitan in its geographies, bringing many places into the singular meditative space of its poems. It is bodily, barbed and evocative: "as if Salome herself, / letting her garment slip, / lowered a breast / to graze his blackened lips" ('Head on a Desert Road'). It is also, in Coleridge's phrase, "less gross than bodily", comprehensive in vision: "everything that this morning was bright / is in shadow, everything is bone that was quick" ('6pm: Coin Du Quai Voltaire: Last Orders'). Artistic exactitude of this kind is rare and rewarding.

Gregory Leadbetter's *Coleridge and the Daemonic Imagination* (Palgrave) won the CCUE Book Prize in 2012. His pamphlet *The Body in the Well* (2007) is published by Happenstance.

℘

Deep In It

PAUL LAFFAN

Janet Rogerson, *A Bad Influence Girl*, £5.50, The Rialto, ISBN 9780955127366;
Edward Mackay, *Swarming*, Salt, £6.50, ISBN 9781844719082;
Tim Liardet, *Madame Sasoo Goes Bathing*, £7, Shoestring Press,
ISBN 9781907356643;
David Harsent, *Songs from the Same Earth*, Rack Press,
£5, ISBN 9780956798190

I once heard the great Scottish theologian and philosopher John McQuarrie say he found poetry very difficult. He had already given out that *The Critique of Pure Reason* was not a very difficult book, but 'To a Skylark' he now confessed had him beaten. Of course, it was a bird!

We could, I assume, have assisted him. Poetry uses the fantastic, the counter-factual, the paradoxical, all for expressive purposes. The skylark is said not to be a bird, since the sublimity of his song appears to make him a being of another order, an inhabitant of heaven (or somewhere near it). Nevertheless I thought of the Professor, reading the poem 'The Madness of Sunshine' in Janet Rogerson's pamphlet when I came upon a line that seemed designed to have rendered him apoplectic: "and the clouds were Western philosophy." What?! Or rather, perhaps, hands off! And I think we might have sided with the Professor on this occasion. I presume the idea is that the clouds move and change and appear impermanent, as some philosophers have spoken of the physical world, but there is nothing surrounding the statement that allows one to be sure. What precedes it is comprehensible and superior:

> The sky was a birdcage
> shadows of gulls haunted the sands

But it does not inform what follows and not all philosophers have thought of the world as in flux. The fantastic must make a kind of sense. Similarly, 'When a Horse Crosses a River' closes:

> The trees, ferns and hills
> exchange looks, they know
> what the horse is thinking
> in the same way they know
> what you are thinking
> when you cross a river.

The trees and hills exchanging looks is a comprehensible, indeed an attractive, conceit, since they stand, we can imagine, in the same space angled towards and away from one another. But that they should know what a horse thinks is another idea and it will have to achieve its own appropriateness if we are to believe it, particularly since in the extension of the landscape's sapience out from the horse to "you", to ourselves as readers, it is suggested there is something about crossing a river which is particularly incursive of thought. Furthermore, the thought that results is clearly supposed to be worth knowing about, not least because it enjoys the emphasis of being what the poem ends with. At the same time, what we have learned of the horse is disqualified from being what this thought is: we could not be fooled by the ripples in the water into believing we are a zebra (another clever idea). So I think we should be told what this thinking is. This may seem prescriptive. But the idea must justify itself somehow if it is not to seem merely arcane, and if the poem is to be a product of something real, rather than just a way of using words.

A quotation from Louise Bourgeois – "When I do not attack I do not feel myself alive" – makes for a rather forbidding epigraph to Edward Mackay's pamphlet and one is politely surprised on learning from the blurb that his other occupation is running a mediation service. The poetry, appropriately, bowls from the epigraphic end and deploys a steely heart. In 'Of or Pertaining to a Raven', an historical tour of the horizon finds the bird to be the great survivor of the mayhem he has sown down the years: "make history with a flap of the wing. Outlast all. I peck and time runs red." "Peck" counterbalances the weight of "time" nicely here and the poem is dense in a positive way, if conceptually a little familiar – something like *Crow* by way of 'Sympathy for the Devil'.

Along with the steeliness – in 'The Abbat' the pleasures of inhabiting an abattoir; in 'Against Gratitude' the imagining of revenge upon a lost partner; and the slightly softened allowances of 'RSVP', about attending an old flame's wedding – there is a sacramental sense that means bread and wine, flesh and blood, are often recurred to. They do not seem, however, to offer much hope: blood and suffering is just what is going on. Mackay's poetry has a strong character, but its nature poses the question of taste and judgement acutely.

Tim Liardet's *Madame Sasoo Goes Bathing* is a pamphlet of poems set on the island of Mauritius. At its centre is a long poem entitled 'At Gris Gris' – a point on the island where a beast of indeterminate type comes ashore. It is "Antarctica's lugubrious stray" and "blubbered for Forty-Below" – a punchy bit of phrasing, in which the alliterations of "blubbered" and "Below" are both internal and enjoyably delayed by the alliteration of "for" and "Forty". So equipped, the beast's appearance at a place of boiling heat is indicative of a wider terrestrial derangement.

If Liardet does not quite seem able to hold himself to the grim portent of the beast's arrival, nor the tensions of a marriage between a – presumably – English man and an Islamic Mauritian woman, it is because relish of the experience of the island is the most powerful force in the poetry. That, plus a sense of humour and a rather kindly disposition, means there is no sense of subjects being pre-picked for their significance. Liardet attends to what the island offers, and in 'The Flame Trees of Trou aux Biches' the simple beauty of the place comes through strongly without feeling forced.

David Harsent's *Songs from the Same Earth* is a cycle of poems put to music by his frequent collaborator, Harrison Birtwhistle, to celebrate Benjamin Britten's centenary. It begins with what struck me as rather Tennysonian cadences: "Silence of slow water, silence of the rose / that burdened the summer...". Very fine they are, but for the addressee of the cycle such calm is past. Whatever exactly it is she is going through, she is deep in it. Harsent offers images that are precise and vivid to gorgeous degree ("when the moon / tipped up on the skyline; when the river / glossed along its length"), but the poetry is so built it remains largely opaque in narrative terms. There is an undertow of loss, and the voice which addresses the woman steps into the cycle in the first and last poems, suggesting the loss concerns what was between the two. At other times, there is the suggestion that the male 'other', so to speak, exists only in the woman's fears, and she receives the reproof: "You wear your victimhood like something cut to fit..." – "victimhood" being the only word in the sequence which seems borrowed from somewhere else and unrenovated. But the collection is compelling and one feels prosaic speculating about what is literally happening in the poems.

Paul Laffan is currently working on a book about the New Testament.

⏤ ℬ ⏤

For Lard's Sake

DAVID WHEATLEY

Raymond Queneau, *Hitting the Streets*, trans. Rachel Galvin, Carcanet, £12.95, ISBN 9781847771575

What is the shortest street in Paris? Who was Père Lachaise? There is one bronze cobblestone in Paris. Where is it located? With such questions Raymond Queneau quizzed the readers of his 'Do You Know Paris?' column in *L'intransigeant* between 1936 and 1938. Queneau's research for his column took the form of a latter-day beating the bounds, that medieval rite of circumambulating the parish to call down blessings on it, and 30 years later he was still feeling the benefits. Introducing *Hitting the Streets*, her translation of his 1967 collection *Courir les rues*, Rachel Galvin recounts the story of Amphion, who constructed the ramparts of Thebes by playing the lyre so well the stones moved and went where he told them. Guillaume Apollinaire designated Amphion the bard of *flâneurs*, and christened his poems *antiopées*. Queneau has more than a touch of Amphion about him in *Hitting the Streets*, with the small difference that where the Greek bard hymned a city into being Queneau celebrates a Paris on the point of disappearance, the picaresque city captured so winningly in his novels *Le chiendent* and *Zazie dans le Métro*. There is a grimmer reaper at work here than the scissors sharpener of 'Future Pasts', in the form of post-war redevelopment. We are, I presume, licensed to find an irony in Queneau lamenting the "abolished residence" of a line of chimney pots in a poem called 'Boulevard Haussmann', Haussmann having spent the mid-nineteenth century flattening what survived of medieval Paris and goading Baudelaire into the ghetto nimbyism of 'Le Cygne' ("*Paris change! mais rien dans ma mélancolie / N'a bougé!*").

Before the dust quite settles, much work remains to be done. These are poems of mythpoeic gusto, answering to animist impulses as deep as the Paris sewers ("*Einai gar kai entautha theous*", runs the epigraph from Heraclitus: "the gods are here also.") Speaking of Apollinaire, that poet features obliquely in 'Rue Pierre-Larousse', which explains the identity of the Comte de Mirabeau thus: "Below his bridge flows the Seine." "*Sous le pont Mirabeau coule la Seine / et nos amours*". *Hitting the Streets* is a love song to urban transience, to the woman undressing spotted from the platform of Passy Métro station and the inscriptions on a *pissoir* wall. In his recent jeremiad against modern life in general, Jonathan Franzen drew a distinction between the urban experience in Latin countries and that of Germany and more Nordic climes. Going to buy a loaf of bread in Lisbon or Florence is an aesthetic pleasure, conventional wisdom tells us, but doing so in Dortmund is not. Queneau's Paris comes with plenty of imported Breton grit (he was born in Le Havre), and the jejune rhapsodies of Breton's *Nadja* are notably absent (Queneau's parting of the ways with the surrealists came early). With his love of mathematics and of that "*dégonfleur d'enflure*" ("detumescer"), Nicolas Boileau, Queneau may cut a forbiddingly rationalist figure. But this is only half the story, the other half being the comedic, Oulipian sower of mayhem that stalks *Hitting the Streets*.

Queneau tends to prefer his humour dry, but herein lurks another of this volume's surprises. If, like me, you have previously suspected Queneau's poems of a certain over-calculated quality (the rather contrived fun of the *Hundred Thousand Billion Poems*), what will most pleasantly surprise about *Hitting the Streets* is its improvised, streetwise feel. "I want a holophrase", wrote Hope Mirrlees in 'Paris: A Poem', incorporating advertising hoardings and the names of Métro stations into her text, and Queneau too is all holophrase, textual rag-picking, and eavesdropped conversations. There is a poem on the 'Loi du 29 juillet 1881' (post no bills), that vain attempt of French officialdom to treat the flaking skin that is the natural state of the urban epidermis. Text overwrites text, streets vanish, and the Roman name for Paris, *Lutetia*, merges with Lethe as "the river of forgetfulness carries away the city":

> the re-baptised streets the torn-down posters
> the river of forgetfulness whose mythological name one even
>   misremembers
> the forgotten Lethe does not cease to flow

The most obvious manifestations of the city as palimpsest are the layers of pigeon droppings on all sides, as noted in 'Cleanliness', whose birds are full of "whimsicrap" ("*fientaisie*"). Flies form storied dynasties though flies today aren't what they were, and human transients turn up, too, in the form of some Tuareg nomads. Queneau is a rambunctious stylist and in Galvin has found a no less rambunctious translator, as the Tuareg challenge confirms. Queneau:

> *Le targui se targuait de tâter de l'orgue*
> *tant il arguait qu'irriguant l'erg*
> *il y ferait nager l'iceberg*
> *cristal des échos sahariens*

Galvin:

> The Tuareg gloated over giving the organ a go
> he swaggered so much that while irrigating the erg
> he set to sea a crystal iceberg
> of Saharan echoes

While the English doesn't manage the sequence of 'a' sounds in the original, the assonating 'o's do a good job in their place with a pleasant slight return on the open vowel of the final "echoes". It gets better, though. Consider 'La tour translatoire', in which we find Queneau exulting in his untranslatability:

> *La Tour Eiffel perd ses cheveux*
> *ce sont les fils de la Vierge*
> *le Christ aussi est fils de la Vierge*
> *allez me traduire ça en Anglais*

"*Fils de la Vierge*" are cobwebs. The pun on "son of the virgin" in the following line is a tall order, but here is Galvin's attempt:

> The Eiffel Tower is losing its hair
> this is a spinster's filamentary issue
> Christ is also the filial issue of a spinster
> go translate that into French for me!

"Spinster" for "spider" is inspired, as is "filamentary issue". By the time we get to the hyper-translation of the last line ("French" for "*Anglais*") Galvin is just rubbing it in. Not everything carries across so fluently: when Montparnasse Station decides to relocate to the New York Museum of Modern Art in *Destin* ('Destination Destiny'), Queneau ends with a squelchy transformation: "*elle se fige comme lard*". "She congeals like lard" doesn't quite do the job, missing the pun on lard/*l'art* and leaving us lard for lard's sake. For the most part though, there is precious little fat on the bones of these translations.

Nominative determinism is the theory that names shape our destinies (*omen est nomen*), thus explaining the high proportion of dentists called Dennis. As chance would have it, the same phenomenon intrudes in this translation when 'Rue Volta' remembers the Italian scientist "whose name gallivanted the circuit/ gallivant gallivant/ galvanised in a jolt on Volta". Queneau the poet has been comprehensively galvanised by Rachel Galvin. One small correction, though. Queneau claims that cities are 'heteronyms', in the sense that there is no rue de Paris in Paris. Not so! There is a rue de Paris off the Boulevard Pérépherique, Ian Duhig informs me. Oh, and the answers to my opening questions: rue des Degrés, which is six metres long; Louis XIV's confessor; and in the Parvis Notre-Dame, where it forms the point of departure for all mileage markers throughout France. Galvin's electrifying translation forms an exemplary point of departure for the rediscovery of Queneau's poetry.

David Wheatley's *A Nest on the Waves* was published by Gallery in 2010.

ॐ

Stammering, Stops, Silence
On the Method and Uses of Untranslation

ANNE CARSON

Each something is a celebration of the nothing that supports it.
— John Cage

Silence is as important as words in the practice and study of translation. This may sound like a cliché. (I think it is a cliché. Perhaps we can come back to cliché.) There are two kinds of silence that trouble a translator: physical, metaphysical. Physical silence happens when you are looking at, say, a poem of Sappho's inscribed on a papyrus from 2,000 years ago that has been torn in half. Half the poem is empty space. A translator can signify or even rectify this lack of text in various ways – with blankness or brackets or textual conjecture – and she is justified in doing so because Sappho did not intend that part of the poem to fall silent. Metaphysical silence happens inside words themselves. And its intentions are harder to define. Every translator knows the point where one language cannot be rendered into another. Take the word cliché. Cliché is a French borrowing, past participle of the verb *clicher*, a term from printing meaning "to make a stereotype from a relief printing surface". It has been assumed into English unchanged, partly because using French words makes English-speakers feel more intelligent and partly because the word has imitative origins (it is supposed to mimic the sound of the printer's die striking the metal) that make it untranslatable. English has different sounds. English falls silent. This kind of linguistic decision is simply a measure of foreignness, an acknowledgment of the fact that languages are not

The Poetry Society Annual Lecture was delivered at the British Museum and as the Kenneth Allott Lecture at the University of Liverpool in September 2013. This essay was first published as 'Variations On the Right to Remain Silent' in *A Public Space*, 7 (2008), and published online at *Poetry Daily*. The variations on the Ibykos fragment appeared as 'A Fragment of Ibykos Translated Six Ways' in *London Review of Books* (8 November, 2012).

algorithms of one another, you cannot match them item for item. But now what if, within this silence, you discover a deeper one – a word that does not intend to be translatable. A word that stops itself. Here is an example.

In the fifth book of Homer's *Odyssey*, when Odysseus is about to confront a witch named Kirke whose practice is to turn men into pigs, he is given by the god Hermes a pharmaceutical plant to use against her magic. Here is Homer's description of it:

> So speaking Hermes gave him the drug
> by pulling it out of the ground and he showed the nature of it:
> at the root it was black but like milk was the flower.
> *MVLU* is what the gods call it. And it is very hard to dig up
> for mortal men. But gods can do such things.   (10.305)

MVLU is one of several occurences in Homer's poems of what Homer regards as a "language of gods". There are a handful of people or things in epic poetry that have this sort of double name. Linguists like to see in these names traces of some older layer of Indo-European preserved in Homer's Greek. However that may be, when he invokes the language of gods Homer usually tells you the earthly translation also. Here he does not. He wants this word to fall silent. Here are four letters of the alphabet, you can pronounce them but you cannot define, possess or make use of them. You cannot search for this plant by the roadside or google it and find out where to buy some. The plant is sacred, the knowledge belongs to gods, the word stops itself. Almost as if you were presented with a portrait of some person – not a famous person but someone you might recognise if you put your mind to it – and as you peer closely you see, in the place where the face should be, a splash of white paint. Homer has splashed white paint not on the faces of his gods but on their word. What does this word hide? We will never know. But that smudge on the canvas does serve to remind us of something important about these puzzling beings, the gods of epic, who are not consistently bigger, stronger, smarter, nicer or better-looking than humans, who are in fact anthropomorphic clichés from top to bottom, yet who do have one escapade up their sleeve – immortality. They know how not to die. And who can say but the four untranslatable letters of MVLU might be the place where that knowledge is hidden.

There is something maddeningly attractive about the untranslatable, about a word that goes silent in transit. I want to explore some examples of this attraction, at its most maddened, from the trial and condemnation of Joan of Arc.

Joan of Arc's history, especially the historical record of her trial, is one fraught with translation at every level. She was captured in battle on 23 May 1430. Her trial lasted from January to May of 1431 and entailed a magistrate's inquest, six public interrogations, nine private interrogations, an abjuration, a relapse, a relapse trial and condemnation. Her death by fire took place on 30 May 1431. Thousands of words went back and forth between Joan and her judges during the months of her inquisition; many of them are availabe to us in some form. But Joan herself was illiterate. She spoke Middle French at her trial, whose minutes were transcribed by a notary and later translated into Latin by one of her judges. This process involved not only the transposition of Joan's direct responses into indirect speech and of her French idioms into the Latin of juridical protocol, but also deliberate falsification of some of her answers in such a way as to justify her condemnation (this criminal intervention was revealed at a retrial that took place 25 years after her death).[1] Yet these many layers of official distance separating us from what Joan said are just an after-effect of the one big original distance that separates Joan herself from her sentences.

All Joan's guidance, military and moral, came from a source she called "voices". All the blame of her trial was gathered up in this question, the nature of the voices. She began to hear them when she was 12 years old. They spoke to her from outside, commanding her life and death, her military victories and revolutionary politics, her dress code and heretical beliefs. During the trial Joan's judges returned again and again to this crux: they insisted on knowing the story of the voices. They wanted her to name, embody and describe them in ways they could understand, with recognisable religious imagery and emotions, in a conventional narrative that would be susceptible to conventional disproof. They framed this desire in dozens of ways, question after question. They prodded and poked and hemmed her in. Joan despised the line of inquiry and blocked it as long as she could. It seems that for her the voices had no story. They were an experienced fact so large and real it had solidifed in her as a sort of sensed abstraction – what Virginia Woolf once called "that very jar on the nerves before it has been made anything".[2] Joan wanted to convey the jar on the nerves without translating it into theological cliché. It is her rage

---

1. F. Meltzer (2001), pp. 119-121.
2. V. Woolf (1927), p. 193.

against cliché that draws me to her. A genius is in her rage. We all feel this rage at some level, at some time. The genius answer to it is catastrophe.

I say catastrophe is an answer because I believe cliché is a question. We resort to cliché because it's easier than trying to make up something new. Implicit in it is the question, Don't we already know what we think about this? Don't we have a formula we use for this? Can't I just send an electronic greeting card or photoshop a picture of what it was like rather than trying to come up with an original drawing? During the five months of her trial Joan persistently chose the term "voice" to describe how God guided her. She did not spontaneously claim that the voices had bodies, faces, names, smell, warmth or mood, nor that they entered the room by the door, nor that when they left she felt sad. Under the inexorable urging of her inquisitors she gradually added all these details. But the storytelling effort was clearly hateful to her and she threw white paint on it wherever she could, giving them responses like:

> ...You asked that before. Go look at the record.
> ...Pass on to the next question, spare me.
> ...I knew that well enough once but I forget.
> ...That does not touch your process.
> ...Ask me next Saturday.

And one day when the judges were pressing her to define the voices as singular or plural, she most wonderfully said (as a sort of summary of the problem):

> The light comes in the name of the voice.

The light comes in the name of the voice is a sentence that stops itself. Its components are simple yet it stays foreign, we cannot own it. Like Homer's untranslatable MVLU it seems to come from somewhere else and it brings a whiff of immortality with it. We know that in Joan's case this turned out to be a whiff of herself burning. Let's pass on to a less dire example of the escapade of translation, but one that is equally driven by the rage against cliché or – as the tranlsator himself in this case puts it – "I want to paint the scream not the horror."[3] This you may recognise as a statement of the painter Francis Bacon in reference to his well known

---

3. D. Sylvester (1987), p.48.

series of portraits of the pope screaming (which are variations on a portrait of Pope Innocent X by Velazquez).

Now Francis Bacon is someone who subjected himself to inquisition repeatedly throughout his career, most notably in a series of interviews with art critic David Sylvester, which are published in *The Brutality of Fact*. "The brutality of fact" is Bacon's own phrase for what he is after in a painting. He is a representational painter. His subjects are birds, dogs, grass, people, sand, water, himself and what he wants to capture of these subjects is their "reality" or (once he used the term) "essence" or (often) "the facts". By "facts" he doesn't mean to make a copy of the subject as a photograph would, but rather to create a sensible form that will translate directly to your nervous system the same sensation as the subject. He wants to paint the sensation of a jet of water, that very jar on the nerves. Everything else is cliché. Everything else is the same old story of how Saint Michael or Saint Margaret or Saint Catherine came in the door with a thousand angels around them and a sweet smell filled the room. He hates all that storytelling, all that illustration, he will do anything to deflect or disrupt the boredom of storytelling, including smudge the canvas with sponges or throw paint at it.

Francis Bacon does not invoke the metaphor of translation when he describes what he wants to do to your nerves by means of paint, but he does at times literally arrive at silence, as when he says to his interviewer, "You see this is the point at which one absolutely cannot talk about painting. It's in the process." In this statement he is making a territorial claim for the untranslatable, as Joan of Arc did when she said to her judges, "That does not touch your process".[4] Two different senses of "process" but the same exasperated shrug toward an authority whose demands are unrealistic. One can sense this exasperation shaping Joan's public life – her military recklessness, her choice of men's clothing, her abjuration of heresy, her relapse into heresy, her legendary final words to the judges: "Light your fires!" Had silence been a possibility for her, Joan would not have ended up in the fires. But the inquisitors' method was to reduce everything she had said to twelve charges in their Latin language and their own wording. That is to say, their story of her solidified as the fact of the matter.[5] The charges were read out to her. She had to answer each with "Yes I believe it" or "No I believe it not". A yes or no question

---

4. M. Peppiatt (1989), p.53.
5. F. Meltzer (2001), p.124.

Study after Velázquez's Portrait of Pope Innocent X, 1953, by Francis Bacon. Oil on canvas, 153 x 118 cm.

forbids a word to stop itself. Untranslatability is illegal.

Stops and silence of various kinds, however, seem to be available to Francis Bacon within the process of his painting: for instance, in his subject matter, when he chooses to depict people screaming in a medium that cannot transmit sound; or in his use of colour, which is a complex matter, but let's look at one aspect of it, namely the edges of the colour. His aim as a painter, as we have seen, is to grant sensation without the boredom of its conveyance. He wants to defeat narrative wherever it seeks to arise, which is pretty much everywhere since humans are creatures who crave a story. There is a tendency for story to slip into the space between any two figures or any two marks on a canvas. Bacon uses colour to silence this tendency. He pulls colour right up to the edge of his figures – a colour so hard, flat, bright, motionless, it is impossible to enter into it or wonder about it. There is a desolation of curiosity in it. He once said he'd like to "put a Sahara desert or the distances of a Sahara" inbetween parts of a painting.[6] His colour has an excluding and accelerating effect, it makes your eye move on. It's a way of saying, don't linger here and start thinking up stories, just stick to the facts. Sometimes he puts a white arrow on top of the colour to speed your eye and denounce storytelling even more. To look at this arrow is to feel an extinguishing of narrative. He says he got the idea for the arrows from a golf manual.[7] To know this makes me feel even more hopeless about understanding the story of his picture. Bacon has no interest in encouraging such hope, nor did Joan of Arc when her inquisitors asked "What do your voices sound like?" and she answered "Ask me next Saturday." Bacon extinguishes the usual relation of figure to ground, the usual passage of information at that place, as Joan extinguishes the usual relation of question to answer. They put a stop on the cliché.

Bacon has another term for this stopping: he calls it "destroying clarity with clarity".[8] Not just in his use of colour but in the whole strategy of his compositions, he wants to make us see something we don't yet have eyes for, to hear something that was never sounded. He goes inside clarity to a place of deeper refreshment, where clarity is the same and yet differs from itself, which may be analogous to the place inside a word where it falls silent in its own presence. And it is noteworthy that for Bacon this is

---

6. D. Sylvester (1987), p.56.
7. H. Davies (1975), p.63.
8. G. Deleuze (2003), p.6.

a place of violence. He talks a lot about violence in his interviews. He gets asked a lot about violence in his interviews. He and his interviewers do not mean the same thing by this word. Their question is about images of crucifixion, slaughtered meat, twisting, mangling, bullfights, glass cages, suicide, half-animals and unidentifiable flesh. His answer is about reality. He is not interested in illustrating violent situations and disparages his own works that do so as "sensational". He wants to convey the sensation not the sensational, to paint the scream not the horror. And he understands the scream in its reality to lie somewhere inside the surface of a screaming person or a screamworthy situation. If we consider his study of the pope screaming alongside the painting that inspired it, Velazquez's *Portrait of Innocent X*, we can see what Bacon has done is to plunge his arms into Velazquez's image of this profoundly disquieted man and to pull out a scream that is already going on there deep inside. He has made a painting of silence in which silence silently rips, as black holes are said to do in deep space when no one is looking. Here is Bacon speaking to David Sylvester:

> When talking about the violence of paint it's nothing to do with the violence of war. It's to do with an attempt to remake the violence of reality itself… and the violence also of the suggestions within the image itself which can only be conveyed through paint. When I look at you across the table I don't only see you, I see a whole emanation which has to do with personality and everything else… the living quality… all the pulsations of a person… the energy within the appearance… And to put that over in a painting means that it would appear violent in paint. We nearly always live through screens – a screened existence. And I sometimes think when people say my work is violent that from time to time I have been able to clear away one or two of the screens.[9]

Bacon says we live through screens. What are these screens? They are part of our normal way of looking at the world, or rather our normal way of seeing the world without looking at it, for Bacon's claim is that a real seer who looked at the world would notice it to be fairly violent – not violent as narrative surface but somehow violently composed underneath

9. D. Sylvester (1987), 82; Deluze (2003), pp.38-9.

the surface, having violence as its essence. No one has ever seen a black hole yet scientists feel confident they can locate its essence in the gravitational collapse of a star – this massive violence, this something which is also, spectacularly, nothing. But let us now shift our historical gaze to Germany at the turn of the eighteenth century and give our attention to a lyric poet of that time, who disappeared into his own black hole while trying to translate the colour purple.

Our English word "purple" comes from Latin *purpureus*, which comes from Greek *PORFURA*, a noun denoting the purplefish. This sea mollusc, properly the purple limpet or murex, was the source from which all purple and red dyes were obtained in antiquity. But the purplefish had another name in ancient Greek, namely *KALXH*, and from this word was derived a verb and a metaphor and a problem for translators. The verb *KALXAINEIN*, "to search for the purplefish", came to signify profound and troubled emotion: to grow dark with disquiet, to seethe with worries, to harbour dark thoughts, to brood in the deep of one's mind. When the German lyric poet Friedrich Hölderlin undertook to translate Sophokles's *Antigone* in 1796, he met this problem on the first page. The play opens with a distressed Antigone confronting her sister Ismene. "What is it?" asks Ismene, then she adds the purple verb. "You are obviously growing dark in mind, brooding deeply ('*kalchainous*') over some piece of news" (*Antigone*, 20). This is a standard rendering of the line. Hölderlin's version, "*Du scheinst ein rotes Wort zu färben*", would mean something like "You seem to colour a reddish purple word, to dye your words red-purple". The deadly literalism of the line is typical of him. His translating method was to take hold of every item of the original diction and wrench it across into German exactly as it stood in its syntax, word order and lexical sense. The result was versions of Sophokles that made Goethe and Schiller laugh aloud when they heard them. Learned reviewers itemised more than one thousand mistakes and called the translations disfigured, unreadable, the work of a madman. Indeed by 1806 Hölderlin was certified insane. His family committed him to a psychiatric clinic, from which after a year he was released as incurable. He spent the remaining 37 years of his life in a tower overlooking the river Neckar, in varying states of indifference or ecstasy, walking up and down his room, playing the piano, writing on scraps of paper, receiving the odd visitor. He died still insane in 1843. It is a cliché to say Hölderlin's Sophokles translations show him on the verge of breakdown and derive their luminous, gnarled, unpronounceable weirdness from his mental condition. Still I wonder what exactly is the relation of madness to translation? Where does translation happen in the mind? And if there is a silence that falls inside certain words, when, how, with what violence does that take place, and what difference does it make to who you are?

One thing that strikes me about Hölderlin as a translator, and about Francis Bacon as a painter, and for that matter about Joan of Arc as a soldier of God, is the high degree of self-consciousness that is present in their respective manipulations of catastrophe. Hölderlin had begun to be preoccupied with translating Sophokles in 1796 but did not publish *Oedipus* and *Antigone* until 1804. Judging his first versions "not living [*lebendig*] enough", he subjected them to years of compulsive revision, forcing the texts from strange to more strange. Here is Hölderlinian scholar David Constantine's description of this effort:

> He warped the original to fit his own idiosyncratic understanding not only of it but also of his obligation in translating it... Choosing always the more violent word, so that the texts are stitched through with the vocabulary of excess... he was also voicing those forces in his own psychology which, very soon, would carry him over the edge. And in uttering them did he not aid and abet them? It is the old paradox: the better the poet says these things, the better he arms them against himself. So well put, are they not irresistible?[10]

Irresistible at least was the process of this violence. For it is remarkable that Hölderlin began at this time to revise also his own early work and he went about it the same way, that is, he would scrutinise finished poems for the "not living enough" parts, then translate these into some other language, also German, that lay silent inside his own. As if he were moving along a line ripping the lids off words and plunging his arms in, he met his madness coming the other way.

Yet it was not altogether a chance meeting. From early on Hölderlin had a theory of himself. This from a letter to his friend Neuffer in 1798, which begins with the sentence, "Livingness [*lebendigkeit*] in poetry is now what most preoccupies my mind", then goes on to this lucid analysis of his own balance of being:

---

10. D. Constantine (2001), pp.8-11.

> because I am more destructible than some other men, I must
> seek all the more to derive some advantage from what has a
> destructive effect on me... I must accept it in advance as
> indispensable material, without which my most inward being
> cannot ever entirely present itself. I must assimilate it, arrange
> it... as shadows to my light... as subordinate tones among
> which the tone of my soul springs out all the more livingly.[11]

This from a letter to Hölderlin's mother from his friend Sinclair in 1804:

> I am not the only one – there are six or eight people besides me
> who have met Hölderlin and are convinced that what appears
> to be mental derangement is in fact nothing of the sort but is
> rather a manner of expressing himself which he has
> deliberately adopted for very cogent reasons.[12]

This from an 1804 review of his Sophokles translations:

> What do you make of Hölderlin's Sophokles? Is the man mad
> or does he just pretend or is his Sophokles a veiled satire on bad
> translators?[13]

Maybe Hölderlin was pretending to be mad the whole time, I don't
know. What fascinates me is to see his catastrophe, at whatever level of
consciousness he chose it, as a method extracted from translation, a
method organised by the rage against cliché. After all what else is one's
own language but a gigantic cacophonous cliché. Nothing has not been
said before. The templates are set. Adam long ago named all the creatures.
Reality is captured. When Francis Bacon approaches a white canvas its
empty surface is already filled with the whole history of painting up to
that moment, it is a compaction of all the clichés of representation already
extant in the painter's world, in the painter's head, in the probability of
what can be done on this surface. Screens are in place making it hard to see
anything but what one expects to see, hard to paint what isn't already
there. Bacon is not content to deflect or beguile cliché by some painterly
trick, he wants to (as Deleuze says in his book about Bacon)

---

11. E. Santner (1990), p.xxix.
12. D. Constantine (2001), pp.116-117, p.381.
13. A. Fioretis (1999), p.277.

"catastrophise" it right there on his canvas. So he makes what he calls "free marks" on the canvas, both at the beginning when it is white and later when it is partly or completely painted. He uses brushes, sponges, sticks, rags, his hand or just throws a can of paint at it. His intention is to disrupt its probability and to shortcircuit his own control of the disruption. His product is a catastrophe, which he will then proceed to manipulate into an image that he can call real. Or he may just hang it up:

> David Sylvester: You would never end a painting by suddenly throwing something at it. Or would you?
> Francis Bacon: Oh yes. In that triptych on the shoulder of the figure being sick into the basin, there's a whip of white paint that goes like that. Well I did that at the very last moment and I just left it.[14]

Free marks are a gesture of rage. One of the oldest myths we have of this gesture is the story of Adam and Eve in the garden of paradise. Eve changes human history by putting a free mark on Adam's apple. Why does she do this? To say she was seduced by the snake or longing for absolute knowledge or in search of immortality are possible answers. On the other hand maybe she was catastrophising. Adam had just performed the primordial act of naming, had taken the first step towards imposing on the wide-open pointless meaningless directionless dementia of the real a set of clichés that no one would ever dislodge, or want to dislodge – they are our human history, our edifice of thought, our answer to chaos. Eve's instinct was to bite this answer in half.

Most of us, given a choice between chaos and naming, between catastrophe and cliché, would choose naming. Most of us see this as a zero sum game – as if there were no third place to be: something without a name is commonly thought not to exist. And here is where we may be able to discern the benevolence of the untranslatable. Translation is a practice, a strategy, or what Hölderlin calls "a salutary gymnastics of the mind",[15] that does seem to give us a third place to be. In the presence of a word that stops itself, in that silence, one has the feeling that something has passed us and kept going, that some possibility has got free. For Hölderlin, as for Joan of Arc, this is a religious apprehension and leads to gods. Francis Bacon doesn't believe in gods but he has a profound relationship with Rembrandt.

---

14. D. Sylvester (1987), p.94.
15. D. Constantine (2001), p.7.

One of his favourite paintings is a self-portrait by Rembrandt. He mentions it in several interviews. What he says he likes about this portrait is that when you go close to it you notice the eyes have no sockets.[16] Perhaps appropriately, I have been unable to find a convincing reproduction of this portrait. It is one of Rembrandt's later darker works, you can hardly make out the contours of the face against background shadow, yet it has a strange power emanating from the socketless eyes. These eyes are not blind. They are engaged in a forceful looking but it is not a look organised in the normal way. Seeing seems to be entering Rembrandt's eyes from the back. And what his look sends forward, in our direction, is a deep silence. Rather like the silence that must have followed Joan of Arc's response to her judges when they asked her, "In what language do your voices speak to you?" and she answered:

Better language than yours.

Or like the silence that covers the final verse of a poem of Paul Celan, which will be our penultimate example of the untranslatable. It is a poem written in praise of Hölderlin and refers to the private language he sometimes spoke during the last 37 years of his life when he was out of his mind or pretending to be so. It is a poem that begins in a movement toward blindness but ends with two socketless eyes that seem to be seeing perfectly well into their own catastrophic little world.

Tübingen, Jänner
Zur Blindheit über-
redete Augen.
Ihre – "ein
Ratsel ist Rein-
entsprungenes" – , ihre
Erinnerung an
schwimmende Hölderlintürme möwen-
umschwirrt.

Besuche ertrunkener Schreiner bei
diesen
tauschenden Wörten.

16. D. Sylvester (1987), pp.56-59; G. Deleuze (2003), p.25.

Käme,
käme ein Mensch,
käme ein Mensch zur Welt heute, mit
den Lichtbart der
Patriarchen: er dürfte,
spräch er von dieser
Zeit, er
dürfte
nur lallen und lallen,
immer-, immer-
zuzu.
("Pallaksch. Pallaksch.")

Tübingen, January
Eyes talked over
to blindness.
Their – "a
riddle is the purely
originated" –, their
memory of
swimming Hölderlintowers, gull-
whirredaround.

Visits of drowned joiners to
these
diving words:

Came,
came a man,
came a man to the world, today, with
the lightbeard of
the prophets: he could,
if he spoke of this
time, he
could
only stammer and stammer,
over-, over-
againagain.
("Pallaksch. Pallaksch.")

This poem is puzzling and dense and has provoked many commentaries. We don't have time here for a detailed analysis but let's focus on the riddles at the beginning and end. At the beginning is a quotation from Hölderlin's poem, 'The Rhine', which is a hymn to the Rhine river. "A riddle is the purely originated" is a sentence that can be read backwards or forwards: origin as riddle or riddle as origin. Whose origin this is, or whose riddle, we are not exactly told. The main action of the poem is a long conditional sentence in the subjunctive – maybe contrafactual maybe not – that seems to lament the powerlessness of language to speak of the times in which we live. A man who chose to struggle with this inadequacy – a prophet or a poet – would be reduced to stammering the same word over and over. Or perhaps further reduced to stammering something that is not quite a word.

According to people who visited him in his tower, Hölderlin invented the term "Pallaksch" and used it to mean sometimes Yes sometimes No. A useful term in that case. Poets are always coming up with these useful terms; they invent neologisms or use existing words in new strange and inventive ways. Of course linguistic invention is a risk. Because it comes across as a riddle and it poses the problem of pure origin: you cannot get behind the back of it, any more than you can find the source of the Rhine or see the sockets in Rembrandt's eyes or know the meaning of the gods' word *MVLU*. "Pallaksch Pallaksch" has to stand as its own clue, has to remain untranslatable. Paul Celan places it in brackets as if he were closing the doors of his poem upon this silence.

To sum up. Honestly, I am not very good at summing up. The best I can do is offer a final splatter of white paint. As a classicist I was trained to strive for exactness and to believe that rigorous knowledge of the world without any residue is possible for us. This residue, which does not exist – just to think of it refreshes me. To think of its position, how it shares its position with drenched layers of nothing, to think of its motion, how it can never stop moving because I am in motion with it, to think of its shadow, which is cast by nothing and so has no death in it (or very little) – to think of these things gives me a sensation of getting free. Let us share this sensation. Here is an exercise, not exactly an exercise in translating, nor even an exercise in untranslating, more like a catastrophising of translation. I shall take a small fragment of ancient Greek lyric poetry and translate it over and over again using the wrong words. A sort of stammering.

The fragment is attributed to Ibykos, a poet of the sixth century BC, known for his love of boys, love of girls, love of adverbs, as well as a general pessimism.

It is a poem about how the poet is affected by the experience of Eros (he's perpetually devastated) whereas other people seem to enjoy a more measured or seasonal reaction. The translations below retain the structure of Ibykos's argument using the template: on the one hand, on the other hand, nay rather, punchline.

[Ibykos fr. 286 PMG]

In spring, on the one hand,
the Kydonian apples trees,
being watered by streams of rivers
where the uncut garden of the maidens [is]
and vine blossoms
swelling
beneath shady vine branches
bloom.
On the other hand, for me
Eros lies quiet at no season.
Nay rather,
like a Thracian north wind
ablaze with lightning,
rushing from Aphrodite
accompanied by parching madnesses,
blackly,
brazenly,
tyrannically,
right up from the bottom of my feet
[it] shakes my whole breathing being.

[Ibykos fr. 286 translated using only words from 'Woman's Constancy' by John Donne]

In woman, on the one hand,
those contracts
being purposed by change and falsehood,
where lovers' images [forswear the persons that we were],
and true deaths
sleeping

beneath true marriages,
antedate.
On the other hand, me
thy vow hast not conquered.
Nay rather,
like that new-made Tomorrow,
now disputing,
now abstaining,
accompanied by Love and his wrath,
truly,
not truly,
if I would,
if I could,
[it] justifies my one whole lunatic escape.

[Ibykos fr. 286 translated using only words from Bertolt Brecht's
FBI file #100-67077]

At a cocktail party attended by known Communists, on the one
    hand,
the subject
being suitably paraphrased as Mr & Mrs Bert Brecht,
where ten years of exile have left their mark,
and beneath 5 copies of file 100-190707,
Charles Laughton
returning to the stage as Galileo,
enters an elevator.
On the other hand, of my name with a hyphen between Eugene
    and Friedrich
the Bureau has no record.
Nay rather,
like the name of a certain Frenchman to whom Charles Laughton
    might send packages,
accompanied by an unknown woman
who spoke to an unknown man,
or accompanied by an unknown man
who spoke to an unknown woman,
and in the event that all the captions are not correct,
please turn to page 307.

[Ibykos fr. 286 translated using only words from p. 47 of *Endgame*
by Samuel Beckett]

In your kitchen, on the one hand,
bright corpses
starting to stink of having an idea,
where one of my legs [is]
and beneath sooner or later
the whole universe
doesn't ring and won't work.
On the other hand, I shouldn't think so.
Nay rather,
like a speck in the void,
pacing to and fro,
accompanied by the alarm,
frankly,
angrily,
impatiently,
not very convinced,
[it] kisses me goodbye. I'm dead. (Pause).

[Ibykos fr. 286 translated using only words from *Conversations
with Kafka* by Gustav Janouch pp.136-7]

In the end, on the one hand, all those who sit behind us at the cash
    desks,
being engaged in the most destructive and hopeless rebellion there
    could ever be,
where everything human [has been betrayed]
and
beneath the burden of existence
stock phrases,
with a gentle indefinable smile,
arouse suspicion.
On the other hand,
one who is afraid should not go into the wood.
Nay rather,
like modern armies,
accompanied by lightly spoken phrases in Czech or German,

fearlessly,
patiently,
unfortunately,
against myself,
against my own limitations and apathy,
against this very desk and chair I'm sitting in,
the charge is clear: one is condemned to life not death.

[fr. 286 translated using stops and signs from the London
Underground]

At the excess fare window, on the one hand, the king's bakers,
ditching old shepherds for new elephants,
where east and west [cross north]
and beneath black friars forbidden from barking in church,
angels
mind the gap.
On the other hand,
a multi-ride ticket does not send me padding southwark.
Nay rather, like the seven sisters
gardening in the British Museum,
accompanied by penalties,
tooting,
turnpiked,
hackneyed,
Kentish,
cockfostered,
I am advised to expect delays all the way to the loo.

[Ibykos fr. 286 translated using only words from *The Owner's
Manual* of my new Emerson 1000W microwave oven pp.17-18]

In hot snacks and appetizers, on the one hand, the soy, barbecue,
    Worcestershire or steak sauce,
being sprinkled with paprika,
where a "browned appearance" [is desirable]
and beneath the magnetron tube
soggy crackers,
wrapped in bacon,

toughen.
On the other hand, a frozen pancake
will not crust.
Nay rather,
like radio waves,
bubbling,
spattering,
accompanied by you rubbing your hands together,
without venting the plastic wrap,
without rearranging the pieces halfway through,
without using the special microwave popper,
[it] will burn your nose right off.

Bibliography
M. Archimbaud, *In Conversation with Francis Bacon* (London, 1993)
M. Blanchot, *Le Part du feu* (Paris, 1949)
D. Constantine, *Hölderlin* (Oxford, 1988)
D. Constantine, *Hölderlin's Sophocles* (Tarset, 2001)
H. Davies, 'Interview with Francis Bacon', *Art in America 63* (Mar/Apr 1975), pp.62-68
G. Deleuze, *Francis Bacon: the logic of sensation*, trans. D.W. Smith (London, 2003)
C. Domino, *Francis Bacon Painter of a Dark Vision*, trans. R. Sharman (London, 1997)
A. Fioretos, *The Solid Letter Readings of Friedrich Hölderlin* (Stanford, 1999)
F. Hölderlin *Sämtlicher Werke*, ed. D.E. Sattler (Frankfurt am Main, 1975-)
F. Hölderlin *Hymns and Fragments*, trans. R. Sieburth (Princeton, 1984)
F. Meltzer, *For Fear of the Fire* (Chicago, 2001)
M. Peppiatt, 'Interview with Francis Bacon', *Art International 8* (1989), pp.43-57
T. Pfau, *Friedrich Hölderlin Essays and Letters on Theory* (Albany, 1988)
J. Russell, *Francis Bacon* (London, 1971)
E. Santner, *Friedrich Hölderlin Hyperion and Selected Poems* (New York, 1990)
D. Sylvester, *The Brutality of Fact: Interviews with Francis Bacon*, 3rd ed.
(London, 1987)
M. Warner, *Joan of Arc The Image of Female Heroism* (New York, 1981)
V. Woolf, *To the Lighthouse* (New York, 1927)

ℬ

Olsie Drik & Rambo Peng

LETTER FROM BERLIN

JOHN HARTLEY WILLIAMS

I've lived in Berlin since 1976. Two occasions for going home presented themselves. I went back to London in 1982, when my first book came out, and scouted the situations vacant. There wasn't much; what there was was a lot of Union Jacks. I don't care much for the Union Jack, and especially not when waved. This was the occasion of the Falklands War and I thought Britain was suffering from a bout of collective hysteria, so I returned to the bosom of the least war-inclined people in Europe.

The second occasion was when the Wall came down. There were 156 kilometres of it; in its finally evolved form it had a tankproof base, one metre eighty wide, panels sixteen centimetres thick, and it was four metres high, capped with a vast pipe, difficult for clutching fingers to grasp. Today it feels like a dream even to me and I built my house on the Wall – well, not on it, but on a section of land across the narrow strip that was patrolled by allied vehicles.

I thought of going home when the Thing came down because I enjoyed living in West Berlin and I could predict what would happen next. I had a privileged life as a teacher; the city had a declining population and we were given considerable tax advantages to remain. The British Council had offices near Zoo Station and they were happy to assist my projects of inviting British poets over for readings, workshops and so forth. The German partner institutions were also happy to support these ventures; it was axiomatic that the Bonn government would underwrite cultural activity in the city, including foreign culture. After reunification, as I foresaw, this willingness vanished and there was a solidarity tax to pay (there still is, incidentally).

With my students, I made a video film about the departure of the allied forces. The building that was HQ to the allied authority, where every quarter the flags were changed, Russian, British, French, American, is now the administrative building of the Free University, where I taught English for 35 years. In 1976, it needed teaching. English was an unknown language in the general population. It was nowhere visible. The movies were in German, the radio was, there were no newspapers or magazines in

English on the news stands. Nobody (except for professors in the university and allied soldiers) could speak it. It was not the dubious lingua franca it has become.

When I arrived at Tempelhof airport therefore (it is now a field for citizens to go windsurfing), I calculated that my only German phrases, *Danke schön* and *Heil Hitler!* would not get me very far. I would have to learn the language. I'd grown out of ordinary methods of study, so I chose the technique of total immersion. Beer, red wine and a bar stool seemed to me to be essential accompaniments to the adult educational process. I was a deaf mute to start with, but I didn't mind. Even when I can think of something interesting to say – and that happens rarely – I generally prefer not to say it and think about how I might have improved on it if I had said it. That's why I'm a writer. But in due course I learned German. I usually describe it as gutter German to indicate the places I learned it in. I remember being in a bar in Wilmersdorf the day John Lennon was shot and saying with fervour: "*Mein Gott, warum haben sie nicht Rod Stewart erschossen?*" The phrase 'forcible ejection' was given a new definition in response to this utterance. Yes, those are the kind of people I associated with.

It's all different now. English is everywhere. I've just been walking through an estate of three- and four-storey apartment buildings, pleasantly surrounded by trees and greensward. It was erected about 40 years ago, and they have suddenly christened it City Village. Notices describing the layout of the "City Village" are everywhere. Why not *Stadt-Dorf*? (And why christen it anyway?) Because everything is now in English. On my favourite department store entrance the other day it said "Mid Season Sale". A hoarding proclaims "Rooftop terrace for sale". A van goes by with "City Clean" on the side. (Or was it "Citi Kleen"?) So many advertisements on television are now in English that my neighbour says she doesn't understand them. You can see movies in the original version, with or without subtitles. English-speaking tourists – you can relax.

You may be wondering about this. Surely that's not a complaint? "Is it not more congenial to have one's native language around one?" Yes and no. I left England in order not to have English around me. It is indeed congenial to sit in a pub with a friend and talk one's own language – but the clichés of public discourse make me anxious. It seems easier to ignore clichés in a foreign language. Unfortunately advertisers' English is now everywhere, even on German television. Turn it on and you can bet there will be a Barbie model shaking her glossy hair at the camera and saying:

"Because you're worth it."

Berlin gets a lot of attention in the British press these days. Boris Johnson came and wrote a piece in the *Telegraph* saying how surprised he was to find lots of friendly young people, not marching around in brown shirts at all. Will Self, who writes a restaurant column, had his trip paid to eat at Borchardt's (a flash restaurant near the Gendarmenmarkt, just off Friedrichstrasse). I could have told him better places to eat. There is a long piece in a recent *TLS* describing the development from 1880 to 1940 of "raw, vigorous, ugly and haphazard" Berlin, the city Mark Twain called 'Chicago on the Spree'.

The Spree is a rather dismal trickle compared to say the Thames or the Tyne, and there is certainly not much that is beautiful about the city. In terms of practicality, however, it is hard to beat, with an excellent public transport system (although the S-Bahn's penchant for breaking down gives commuters plenty to think about), a grid of cycle ways, wide streets for better traffic flow, and an abundance of green, especially in the west of the city, where tree planting programmes were always vote-winners for politicians. The rawness of the Berliners is worth noting, however. *Die Berliner Schnauze* (the Berlin Mouth) refers to the dry, sometimes acid humour of the local populace (and of course to their dialect). They are direct where Londoners are evasive and the room for misunderstandings is great. I recall a black woman poet I had invited for readings being indignant that a shopkeeper had drawn down the blind of the shop and turned the OPEN sign to CLOSED as the poet was about to enter. "Berliners are racist!" she cried. But it was six o'clock, closing time (in those days at any rate), and Berliners don't wait. I failed to persuade the poet that this gesture was not directed at her personally; it was what Berliners do. They beat you to the newly-opening up check-out at the supermarket, or the last seat on the bus. There's nothing you can do about it.

Berlin has a new airport to replace Tegel (the old West Berlin airport). It's at Schoenefeld, where the former GDR airport still plays host to Easyjet and Ryanair. The new airport has been there for a couple of years already (next to the old one) but is not yet in service because of typical German incompetence. (I hope that phrase surprises you.) If you arrive at the old Schoenefeld you will probably take the S-Bahn into town and you may be struck by the graffiti. Olsie Drik and Rambo Peng have scrawled their logo everywhere. There's more graffiti than there are poems in anthologies; how did they get up there to do that, you ask yourself.

Once in the city, to get a really good idea of the city, I'd suggest riding the S-Bahn ring, clockwise and then anti-clockwise. From Westkreuz to Westkreuz it takes an hour, above ground mostly, not like the Circle Line, so you'll see the two cities in one. Going clockwise you'll circle north to Westhafen where a mighty building proclaims across the skyline: BEHALA BEHALA BEHALA. Chant it to yourself by all means and the force will be with you. (It stands for Berliner Hafen und Lagerhaus Betriebe). Did you ever want to see real dilapidation? Whole buildings of shattered glass and filthy brick have been given the treatment here by Olsie and Rambo, not to mention Wiggi Peniz and all the other sprayers; you are in East Berlin. Get off at Treptower Park and go to the Russian war memorial. Reflect that this stupendous monument celebrates a conquest (and sacrifice) by an invader. Get back on the train and travel south into Sonnenallee and Neukölln – these are the poor districts of West Berlin, and they look smart compared to what you've left behind.

My favourite part of downtown Berlin (City West as they call it) is Savignyplatz. I used to drink with Ken Smith in a pub we called The Fat Landlady (*Die Dicke Wirtin*). Right next to it there used to be the Autorenbuchhandlung, the sort of bookshop people like you and me go to. (It is now located under the S-bahn station – and by the way Berlin is the place for bookshops, London a book-desert in comparison.) I remember the French American writer Raymond Federman giving a reading there. Lovely man. My students and I included him in a film and I remember him telling the student interviewer that he had just spoken to his daughter in New York who told him the epitaph they would write on his tombstone would be: Out of Print.

My fate as well, I suspect.

Berlin, September 2013

Walking with Simon

GRETA STODDART

It's been the hottest August in years. But when I arrive in Crackington Haven on the north Cornish coast a cloud sits like a giant grey cushion above the cove. It's the first day of autumn. First day back at school. Out over the Atlantic the sky is lighter, with pale smudges of blue and sun, but there's a dark heathery steepness to the cliffs. It starts to rain.

I'm not sure if Simon's pleased to see me. It's his first day alone in the 13 days he's been walking. Not so much lone troubadour then as Pied Piper. But he's well in his stride, pumping up and down the relentless peaks and troughs of the South West Coast Path. On my way to meet him I fell into step with a couple from Surrey. When I told them why I was there – to meet the poet Simon Armitage who's walking the coastal path, reading his poems along the way – a small frown of recognition passed over the man's face. Simon is one of the few poets who people with no interest in poetry have heard about. He gets around. It isn't surprising then to hear that he is met with great warmth and hospitality on these walks. When I wonder what would happen if an unknown poet did what he's doing Simon cries out, "Let him try it!"

But I want to know – would a troubadour of the twelfth century be known to the folk in the tavern he pitched up in? Would he have to prove his worth before he was offered some grub, let alone entry? Simon's reputation goes before him, and it's that as much as anything that has opened doors. At the end of *Walking Home* (the book he wrote following a similar experience taking the Pennine Way) he marvels, "I was made welcome wherever I travelled... could any more validation be expected or hoped for?" But I can't help seeing my unknown travelling poet – of both twelfth and twenty-first centuries – knocking on doors, soaked through and stinking, asking to be heard, asking for a bed – and getting short shrift. While I muse on this image Simon points out that the troubadour would have got work, and a welcome, by word of mouth, hearsay. Talk of his talent would have spread from village to village. So Simon's experience may be more like the original troubadour's than the sorry one of my imagination.

In some ways these walks do live out the off-the-cuff, on-the-hoof tradition of poetry that goes back to the itinerant nature of some early poets. After a long day's walking he reads his poems, sometimes to just a handful of people, in schools, bookshops, front rooms. At the end he passes round a sock and people put in what they think he's worth: a tenner, 23p, a ketchup sachet or – my favourite – a mobile number on a scrap of paper, "Brenda. Call me!"

Simon sees poetry as a kind of passport: it gets you "in with the good people", by which I understand those with a ready heart and an open mind, willing to engage and listen, as well as invite you into their homes.

So is this poetry finding itself in the out-of-the-way places, right at the heart of things, being what it always was – a living thing among living people? Simon calls it "taking poetry for a walk". He wants to see if people think an evening spent listening to poems is a good night out. And? It's not about numbers, he says, it's about the quality of the listening of those who come – and they do come.

"I write for people who listen, who concentrate, who make an effort to understand. I want to tell, to communicate. Poetry is already an obscure art. We mustn't forget that when most people are given a poem to read they find it difficult. So poems that are obscure are being doubly so. But some people write like that (and I sometimes enjoy reading those poems), they find themselves in a corner writing and communicating in a way that feels right and true to them; that is how they are in, and how they see, the world. That's fine. But that's not what I want to do."

Simon believes more and more in the return of poetry to the public space – the campfire, temple, theatre. A telling, listening space. The book, he says, sitting on a rock on a blustery beach, waving a map which I take to be an imaginary slim volume, is only the literary incarnation of poetry – implying that it has somehow been confined by that form and that the older, performed, nature of poetry is one in which he is more comfortable. He feels his poetry takes its place in the direct, storytelling line of Hardy, Tennyson, Chaucer. He wants to tell stuff. Think of his recent versions of *Sir Gawain and the Green Knight*, *King Arthur* and his latest book of poems, *Seeing Stars*, with its strange cast of brilliant talkers. And it's that strong speaking voice you hear so clearly in *Walking Home*. Reading it you're walking with him, he's there nattering away in your ear. The prose – I want to say "talk" – has all the direct, lived feel of his poems but is more indulgent, digressive, personal, funny. There's more room for him to wander round, point things out, mull them over. Much more room – nearly 300 miles of room – in meadow, moorland, cliff, bog, field, and path.

He seems to revel in the space prose gives him. Not novels though. He wrote two and it felt too much like a proper job. And I don't want one of those, he says.

On day four of Simon's walk Seamus Heaney died. He found out in a text from a local journalist. With Ted Hughes and Heaney gone, he says – well, who's left? They, especially Heaney, were the last of the Magi, the Wise Men. He doesn't think we'll have more like them, and suggests there may no longer be the need. I don't believe that. I suggest that each generation of poets must feel, when a significant older poet dies, bereft of their poetic mother or father. A bleak, lonely silence ahead. What do you think Heaney felt when Auden died? And Auden when Yeats went? Read his elegy. (I can't help thinking Elizabeth Bishop wrote an elegy for her poetic mother while the latter was still very much alive in the invocatory 'Invitation to Miss Marianne Moore'.) And partly because I want to cheer him up and partly because we are surrounded by some truly impressive geological structures, I say that maybe he is the next layer, or part of the next stratum, in the great sedimentary rock of poetry.

He's got to get on. Boscastle beckons, and with it a night in a witchcraft museum.

There's always a sense of pathos when you watch someone walk away from you, but its particular effect depends on what surrounds them; what the person is walking away *into* somehow brings into relief what they are walking away *from*. In a city a person walks off and they are soon lost in the crowds and traffic, in human space. When you see them recede along a narrow path through heather and gorse and rocks, up huge shale cliffs to the top of a gale-driven brow, you get more of a sense of that person alive on this physical hunk of rock we call earth, earth as planet, planet as a ball in space.

As I watch Simon walk away I think of the title poem in his first collection:

> It begins as a house, an end terrace
> in this case
>   but it will not stop there
> [...]
>   and before we know it it is out of our hands:
> city, nation,
>   hemisphere, universe, hammering out in all directions...
>   ('Zoom!')

I remember that his original impulse three years ago was to "get out of the office and into the wider world again, to rejoin the adventure"; or, to use Robert Louis Stevenson's words, as he does, "to get down off this feather bed of civilisation, and find the globe granite underfoot and strewn with cutting flints".

I sit on Bray's Point above Crackington Haven and as I watch Simon get smaller and smaller I think of the poem Heaney wrote after Hughes died:

> Now it seems
> I'm standing on a pierhead watching him
> All the while watching me as he rows out
> And a wooden end-stopped stern
> Labours and shimmers and dips,
> Making no real headway.
>
> ('Stern')

I look at all the different layers in the rock beneath his walking feet. Down below the waves are coming in to shore and I see how like the layers in the rock they are – the same wavery edges, the same almost regular intervals – but they're alive, in motion, coming in and in at the earth, insisting on themselves. The waves don't stop. They can't. But the layers in the rock are utterly stopped. They're done with their great moving. Both the waves and the rock will go on forever. I squint up to see if I can still see Simon and there he is at the cliff top. He gives a last wave, and is gone.

September 2013

Contributors

Liz Berry's first collection will be published by Chatto & Windus in 2014. **Kate Bingham**'s second collection, *Quicksand Beach* (Seren, 2006), was shortlisted for the Forward Prize. **Robyn Bolam**'s *New Wings: Poems 1977-2007* is published by Bloodaxe. She participated in the University of Southampton's Litmus Project that links arts and sciences. **Jonathan Edwards**'s first collection, *My Family and Other Superheroes,* will be published by Seren in 2014. **Paul Farley**'s *Selected Poems* is due from Picador in 2014. **Matthew Francis**'s fifth collection, *Muscovy,* is published by Faber. **Mir Mahfuz Ali** was born in Dhaka, Bangladesh. His poems have appeared widely in magazines and in *Ten: New Poets from Spread the Word* (Bloodaxe, 2010). **John McAuliffe**'s third collection, *Of All Places* (Gallery, 2011), was a PBS Recommendation. **Stephen McNeilly** is a London based writer, editor and curator. **Kim Moore**'s *If We Could Speak Like Wolves* was a winner in the 2012 Poetry Business Pamphlet Competition. **Helen Mort**'s first collection, *Division Street*, is published by Chatto & Windus. **Diana Pooley**'s first collection, *Like This,* was published by Salt in 2009. **Sheenagh Pugh**'s next collection *Short Days, Long Shadows* is due from Seren in 2014. **Tom Sleigh** is an American poet. He has published seven collections, including *Space Walk* (Houghton Mifflin, 2007), which received the Kingsley Tufts Award. **Gerard Smyth**'s seventh collection, *The Fullness of Time: New and Selected Poems,* was published by Dedalus in 2010. **Greta Stoddart**'s most recent collection is *Salvation Jane* (Anvil, 2008). *At Home in the Dark* (Anvil) received the Geoffrey Faber Award in 2002. **Jack Underwood**'s first collection is due from Faber in 2015. **Susan Wicks**'s *Talking Vrouz*, translations of poems by Valerie Rouzeau, is published by Arc and is a PBS Recommended Translation. **Neil Wenborn**'s collection *Firedoors* (2004) is published by Rockingham Press. **Howard Wright**'s first collection, *King of Country* (2010), was published by Blackstaff. His pamphlet *Blue Murder* appeared from Templar in 2011. **John Hartley Williams**'s novel *Death Comes for the Poets,* co-written with Matthew Sweeney, was published by The Muswell Press in 2012.

ॐ

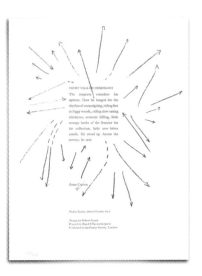

The Corneliu M Popescu Prize
2013
FOR POETRY TRANSLATED FROM A EUROPEAN LANGUAGE INTO ENGLISH

Alice
Oswald
Memorial

The Poetry Society and judges Karen Leeder and David Wheatley
congratulate **Alice Oswald**, the winner of the 2013 Popescu Prize, for her book
Memorial – "an excavation of Homer's *Iliad*" – published by Faber.

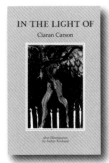

The Poetry Society congratulates all of the poets,
their translators and publishers shortlisted for the prize. Find out more at
www.poetrysociety.org.uk/content/competitions/popescu/